Anonymous

**Church Book**

Containing the Sacramental Offices of the Reformed Dutch Church

Anonymous

**Church Book**
*Containing the Sacramental Offices of the Reformed Dutch Church*

ISBN/EAN: 9783337297367

Printed in Europe, USA, Canada, Australia, Japan

Cover: Foto ©Lupo / pixelio.de

More available books at **www.hansebooks.com**

# Church Book:

CONTAINING THE

## SACRAMENTAL OFFICES

OF THE

### Reformed Dutch Church;

TOGETHER WITH OTHER OFFICES FOR CHRISTIAN SERVICE.

New-York:
CHARLES SCRIBNER & CO., 654 BROADWAY.
1866.

# Index.

|    |    | PAGE |
|----|----|------|
| 1. | Order of Worship on the Lord's Day, | 7 |
| 2. | Order of Scripture Reading, | 14 |
| 3. | Office for Holy Baptism, | 17 |
| 4. | Office for the Celebration of the Lord's Supper, | 25 |
| 5. | Office for the Confirmation of Marriage, | 36 |
| 6. | Office for the Burial of the Dead, | 41 |
| 7. | Form for Ordaining Elders and Deacons, | 50 |
| 8. | Sentences to be used during the Collection of Alms, | 58 |
| 9. | Christian Prayers, | 61 |
| 10. | The Litany, | 63 |
| 11. | Prayers, | 67 |
| 12. | Ancient Christian Hymns and Selections from the Psalter for Chanting, | 77 |
| 13. | Responses to the Decalogue, | 87 |
| 14. | Historical Note, | 88 |

# Preface.

This manual has been prepared at the request of the Consistory of the Church of which the Compiler is Minister, and is issued by them for the use of the Congregation. It contains the Sacramental Offices of the Reformed Dutch Church; the use of this part of our Liturgy by the Churches, being with great propriety, made imperative. These Sacramental Offices cannot be surpassed for clear statement of scriptural truth and for simple, beautiful order. The same is true of the form for Ordaining Elders and Deacons. To these are added such other offices for Christian Service as have been found useful by us. A few words explanatory of these may not be undesirable.

The order of Scripture reading has been carefully prepared with the hope of bringing a larger proportion of Holy Scripture into profitable public use.

The Office for Marriage is slightly altered from that prepared from the liturgies of the Reformed Churches, by the late eminent and beloved Rev. George W. Bethune, D.D.

The Burial Service contains selections from Holy Scripture and suitable prayers; the world-famous hymn of Notker, a Swiss ecclesiastic, who died about A.D. 912, "In the midst of life," etc.; and the form of interment, taken partly from Herman's Reformation Book of Cologne, the ritual portion of which was by

Bucer and the doctrinal by Melancthon, partly from the ancient Salisbury ritual and partly from Holy Scripture.

The Sentences from Scripture to be used during the thank-offering of alms, are such as may instruct and impel in this Christian duty.

Such prayers have been added from our own and other Liturgies of the ancient or reformed churches, as may, without impeding the freedom of extemporaneous devotional utterance, suggest to and at times help it.

And finally, are added Selections for Chanting from the Psalter and ancient Christian hymns, such as belong to the whole Church of Christ.

To a history, than which none is nobler, our ancestral Church has added, as the heirloom of her children, a clear and scriptural confession of her Christian faith; a catechism of the heart, which contains a transcript of true Christian life and experience; and a liturgical usage which blends seemly order with well-directed but never hindered Christian freedom. This manual is intended to help her children to realize her true distinctive position, and to fulfil under her training their service of obedient love to Christ.

NEW-YORK, 1866.

# Order of Public Worship.

## Lord's Day Morning.

### I.

*After a space for private devotion, the Minister shall introduce the public worship by invoking the Divine presence and blessing.*

#### INVOCATION.

#### THE LORD'S PRAYER.

Our Father which art in heaven, Hallowed be Thy name: Thy kingdom come: Thy will be done on earth as it is in heaven: Give us this day our daily bread: And forgive us our debts, as we forgive our debtors: And lead us not into temptation, but deliver us from evil: For Thine is the kingdom, and the power, and the glory, for ever. Amen.

## II.

### SALUTATION.

The peace of God which passeth all understanding keep your hearts and minds through Christ Jesus. Amen.

Or this.

Grace be unto you, and peace from God our Father and from the Lord Jesus Christ. Amen.

Or this.

The grace of our Lord Jesus Christ be with you all. Amen.

## III.

### READING OF SCRIPTURE.

#### I.—The Ten Commandments.

Hear the law of God as it is written in the twentieth chapter of the book of Exodus.

God spake all these words, saying, I am the Lord thy God, which have brought thee out of the land of Egypt, out of the house of bondage.

#### I.

Thou shalt have no other gods before me.

#### II.

Thou shalt not make unto thee any graven image, or any likeness of any thing that is in heaven above, or that is in the earth beneath, or that is in the water under the earth: thou shalt not bow down thyself to them, nor serve them: for I the Lord thy God am a jealous God, visiting the iniquity of the fathers upon the children unto the third and fourth generation of them that hate me; and showing mercy unto thousands of them that love me, and keep my commandments.

### III.

Thou shalt not take the Name of the Lord thy God in vain; for the Lord will not hold him guiltless that taketh His Name in vain.

### IV.

Remember the Sabbath-day to keep it holy. Six days shalt thou labor, and do all thy work: but the seventh day is the Sabbath of the Lord thy God: in it thou shalt not do any work, thou, nor thy son, nor thy daughter, thy man-servant, nor thy maid-servant, nor thy cattle, nor thy stranger that is within thy gates: for in six days the Lord made heaven and earth, the sea, and all that in them is, and rested, the seventh day: wherefore the Lord blessed the Sabbath-day, and hallowed it.

### V.

Honor thy father and thy mother: that thy days may be long upon the land which the Lord thy God giveth thee.

### VI.

Thou shalt not kill.

### VII.

Thou shalt not commit adultery.

### VIII.

Thou shalt not steal.

### IX.

Thou shalt not bear false witness against thy neighbor.

### X.

Thou shalt not covet thy neighbor's house, thou shalt not covet thy neighbor's wife, nor his man-servant, nor his maid-servant, nor his ox, nor his ass, nor any thing that is thy neighbor's.

Hear also what our Lord Jesus Christ saith.

*St. Matthew xxii : 37–40.*

Thou shalt love the Lord thy God with all thy heart, and with all thy soul, and with all thy mind. This is the first and great commandment. And the second is like unto it, Thou shalt love thy neighbor as thyself. On these two commandments hang all the law and the prophets.

Responsive Chant.\*

### II.—FROM THE OLD TESTAMENT.

Responsive Chant.†

### III.—FROM THE NEW TESTAMENT.

### IV.
### SINGING.

### V.
### PRAYER.

---

\* See page 87.   † See page 77.

## VI.
## SINGING.

## VII.
## SERMON.

## VIII.
## PRAYER.

## IX.
## COLLECTION OF ALMS.*

## X.
## SINGING,
### WITH DOXOLOGY.

## XI.
## APOSTOLIC BENEDICTION.

* See page 58.

## Lord's Day Evening.

In the Evening Service of the Lord's Day the Ten Commandments shall be omitted from the Scripture reading.
After the portion from the Old Testament has been read, a short responsive chant may be sung.*
After the portion from the New Testament has been read, unless the Minister shall announce another hymn, the following ancient Christian hymn may be sung:

### GLORIA IN EXCELSIS.

GLORY be to God on high, and on earth peace, goodwill towards men. We praise Thee, we bless Thee, we worship Thee, we glorify Thee, we give thanks to Thee for Thy great glory, O Lord God, heavenly King, God the Father Almighty.

O Lord, the only-begotten Son, Jesus Christ; O Lord God, Lamb of God, Son of the Father, that takest away the sins of the world, have mercy upon us. Thou that takest away the sins of the world, have mercy upon us. Thou that takest away the sins of the world, receive our prayer. Thou that sittest at the right hand of God the Father, have mercy upon us.

\* See page 77.

For Thou only art holy; Thou only art the Lord; Thou only, O Christ, with the Holy Ghost, art most high in the glory of God the Father. AMEN.

<sub>After which shall be said, by the Minister and People standing,</sub>

## THE APOSTLES' CREED.

I BELIEVE IN GOD THE FATHER ALMIGHTY, MAKER OF HEAVEN AND EARTH;

AND IN JESUS CHRIST, HIS ONLY SON OUR LORD, WHO WAS CONCEIVED BY THE HOLY GHOST, BORN OF THE VIRGIN MARY, SUFFERED UNDER PONTIUS PILATE, WAS CRUCIFIED, DEAD, AND BURIED; HE DESCENDED INTO HELL; THE THIRD DAY HE ROSE AGAIN FROM THE DEAD; HE ASCENDED INTO HEAVEN, AND SITTETH ON THE RIGHT HAND OF GOD THE FATHER ALMIGHTY; FROM THENCE HE SHALL COME TO JUDGE THE QUICK AND THE DEAD.

I BELIEVE IN THE HOLY GHOST; THE HOLY CATHOLIC CHURCH; THE COMMUNION OF SAINTS; THE FORGIVENESS OF SINS; THE RESURRECTION OF THE BODY, AND THE LIFE EVERLASTING. AMEN.

## II.

# Order for Reading of Scripture

### in

## Public Worship.

| Lord's Day. | MORNING SERVICE. | | EVENING SERVICE. | |
| --- | --- | --- | --- | --- |
| | OLD TEST. | NEW TEST. | OLD TEST. | NEW TEST. |

### JANUARY.*

| | OLD TEST. | NEW TEST. | OLD TEST. | NEW TEST. |
| --- | --- | --- | --- | --- |
| 1. | Gen. 12 : 1–9 | Romans 8 : 1–17 | Psalm 1 | Luke 2 : 21–40 |
| 2. | " 18 | " 8 : 24–39 | " 8 | Matthew 3 |
| 3. | " 15 | " 10 | " 16 | Luke 4 : 1–13 |
| 4. | " 18 : 16–33 | " 12 | " 19 | Matthew 5 : 1–16 |

### FEBRUARY.

| 1. | Gen. 19 : 12–26 | Romans 15 : 1–21 | Psalm 20 | Matthew 6 : 1–18 |
| --- | --- | --- | --- | --- |
| 2. | " 22 : 1–19 | 1 Corin. 2 | " 23 | " 6 : 19–34 |
| 3. | " 28 | " 12 : 1–27 | " 24 | " 7 : 7–29 |
| 4. | " 32 : 6–32 | " 13 | " 26 | Luke 7 : 11–23 |

### MARCH.

| 1. | Gen. 48 : 8–22 | 2 Corin. 4 | Psalm 32 | Luke 7 : 36–50 |
| --- | --- | --- | --- | --- |
| 2. | " 49 : 1–28 | " 5 | " 34 | Mark 4 : 1–20 |
| 3. | Exod. 6 : 1–13 | " 12 : 1–10 | " 40 | Matt. 11 : 20–30 |
| 4. | " 12 : 21–36 | Galat. 1 | " 41 | Luke 13 : 10–22 |

### APRIL.

| 1. | Exod. 14 : 8–31 | Galat. 3 : 13–29 | Psalm 42 | Luke 18 : 23–35 |
| --- | --- | --- | --- | --- |
| 2. | " 15 : 1–21 | " 4 : 19–31 | " 46 | Mark 9 : 1–13 |
| 3. | " 17 | " 5 | " 51 | Matt. 14 : 22–36 |
| 4. | " 23 : 15–33 | " 6 | " 57 | " 15 : 21–39 |

* When there shall be a fifth Lord's Day in the month, for the proper portion of Scripture, see Table marked Supernumerary, on page 16.

## MAY.

| | MORNING SERVICE. | | EVENING SERVICE. | |
|---|---|---|---|---|
| | OLD TEST. | NEW TEST. | OLD TEST. | NEW TEST. |
| 1. | Exod. 32:1-14 | Ephes. 2 | Psalm 66 | Matt. 18:1-14 |
| 2. | " 33:1-19 | " 3 | " 69 | " 19:18-30 |
| 3. | Num. 17 | " 4 | " 80 | " 22:1-14 |
| 4. | " 20 | " 5 | " 84 | " 25:31-46 |

## JUNE.

| | | | | |
|---|---|---|---|---|
| 1. | Deut. 6:4-25 | Ephes. 6 | Psalm 87 | John 3:1-21 |
| 2. | " 11:10-32 | Philip. 1 | " 94 | " 4:1-26 |
| 3. | " 32:1-14 | " 2 | " 103 | " 6:1-11 |
| 4. | " 33:1-29 | " 3 | " 130 | " 10:1-18 |

## JULY.

| | | | | |
|---|---|---|---|---|
| 1. | Josh. 3:7-17 | Coloss. 1 | Isaiah 35 | John 12:20-36 |
| 2. | " 20 | " 2 | " 40:9-31 | " 14 |
| 3. | " 24:1-25 | " 3 | " 43:1-13 | " 15 |
| 4. | Judg. 5 | " 4 | " 52 | " 16 |

## AUGUST.

| | | | | |
|---|---|---|---|---|
| 1. | 1 Saml. 3 | 1 Thess. 2 | Isaiah 54 | Mark 14:22-45 |
| 2. | " 17:32-54 | " 5 | " 55 | " 14:53-72 |
| 3. | 2 Saml. 6:1-15 | 2 Thess. 1 | " 61 | John 19:1-22 |
| 4. | " 18:9-33 | " 3 | " 62 | Luke 23:34-49 |

## SEPTEMBER.

| | | | | |
|---|---|---|---|---|
| 1. | 2 Sam. 24:10-25 | 1 Tim. 1 | Isaiah 63 | Matt. 27:50-60 |
| 2. | 1 Kgs. 3:5-15 | " 6 | Jerem. 2:1-13 | " 28:1-15 |
| 3. | " 17 | 2 Tim. 1 | " 9:1-11 | Luke 24:13-35 |
| 4. | " 19:21-46 | " 2 | " 17:1-14 | Acts 1:1-14 |

## OCTOBER.

| | MORNING SERVICE. | | EVENING SERVICE. | |
|---|---|---|---|---|
| | OLD TEST. | NEW TEST. | OLD TEST. | NEW TEST. |
| 1. | 1 Kgs. 19 | 2 Tim. 8 | Jerem. 31 : 27–40 | Acts 4 : 18–31 |
| 2. | " 22 : 7–38 | " 4 | " 33 : 1–16 | " 9 : 1–20 |
| 3. | 2 Kgs. 6 : 1–23 | Hebrews 1 | Ezekiel 33 : 1–11 | " 13 : 14–43 |
| 4. | " 17 : 6–23 | " 2 | " 34 : 11–31 | " 16 : 9–33 |

## NOVEMBER.

| | | | | |
|---|---|---|---|---|
| 1. | 2 Kgs. 19 : 8–37 | Heb. 10 : 1–25 | Ezekiel 37 : 1–14 | Acts 17 : 16–34 |
| 2. | " 23 : 1–23 | 1 Peter 1 | Daniel 6 : 1–23 | " 20 : 17–38 |
| 3. | " 25 : 1–21 | " 2 | Hosea 14 | " 21 : 1–14 |
| 4. | 2 Chr. 36 : 5–21 | " 4 | Joel 2 : 12–32 | " 22 : 1–22 |

## DECEMBER.

| | | | | |
|---|---|---|---|---|
| 1. | Ezra 8 | 2 Peter 1 | Micah 6 : 1–8 | Acts 24 : 10–27 |
| 2. | Neh. 3 : 9–18 | 1 John 3 | Zechar. 13 | " 26 |
| 3. | Esther 4 | " 4 | Malachi 3 | " 27 : 21–44 |
| 4. | Job 5 ; 6–27 | " 5 | " 4 | " 28 : 17–31 |

## SUPERNUMERARY.
When there shall be a fifth Sunday in the month.

| | | | |
|---|---|---|---|
| Gen. 47 : 1–12 | 2 Corin. 1 | Psalm 28 | Luke 4 : 14–32 |
| Levit. 26 : 1–20 | Ephes. 1 | " 65 | Mark 4 : 26–41 |
| Judg. 6 : 19–40 | Titus 2 | Eccles. 12 : 1–7 | John 8 : 12–30 |
| 2 Kgs. 2 : 1–15 | James 1 | Song of Solom. 2 : 3–17 | " 18 : 1–17 |
| Job 14 | " 4 | Jonah 3 | Revel. 22 |

| LORD'S SUPPER. | PENTECOST. |
|---|---|
| Isaiah 53 \| John 17 : 15–26 | Deuter. 26 \| Acts 2 : 1–21 |
| BAPTISMAL. | THANKSGIVING. |
| Isaiah 44 : 1–8 \| Romans 6 : 3–14 | Psalm 116 \| Philipp. 4 |
| GOOD-FRIDAY. | |
| Psalm 22 \| Hebrews 2 : 9–18 | CHRISTMAS. |
| EASTER-SUNDAY. | Isaiah 11 : 1–10 \| Luke 2 : 7–20 |
| Isaiah 25 : 1–9 \| John 20 : 1–18 | |

## III.

## THE SACRAMENTS.

### The Office for the Administration of Holy Baptism.

THE principal parts of the doctrine of Holy Baptism are these three :

*First.* That we with our children are *conceived and born in sin*, and therefore (are children of wrath, insomuch that we) cannot enter into the Kingdom of God, except we are born again. [This, the dipping in or sprinkling with water teaches us, whereby the impurity of our souls is signified, and we are admonished to loathe and humble ourselves before God, and seek for our purification and salvation without ourselves.]

*Secondly.* Holy Baptism witnesseth and sealeth unto us *the washing away of our sins* through Jesus Christ. Therefore we are baptized IN THE NAME OF THE FATHER, AND OF THE SON, AND OF THE HOLY GHOST. [For when we are baptized in the name of the FATHER, God the Father witnesseth and sealeth unto us, that He doth make an eternal covenant of grace with us, and adopts us for His children and heirs, and therefore will provide us with every good thing, and avert all evil or turn it to our profit. And when we are baptized in the name of the SON, the Son sealeth unto us that He doth wash us in His blood from all our sins, incorporating us into the fellowship of His death and resurrection, so that we are freed from all our sins and accounted righteous before God. In like manner, when we are baptized in the name of the HOLY GHOST, the Holy Ghost assures us, by this holy sacrament, that He will dwell in us, and sanctify us to be members of Christ, applying unto us that which we have in Christ, namely, the washing away of our sins and the daily renewing of our lives, till we shall finally be presented without spot or wrinkle among the assembly of the elect in life eternal.]

*Thirdly.* Whereas in all covenants there are contained two parts, therefore are we by God, through Baptism, *admonished of, and obliged unto new obedience*, namely, that we cleave to this one God, Father, Son, and Holy Ghost; that we trust in Him and love Him with all our heart, with all our soul, with all our mind, and with all our strength; that we forsake the world, crucify our old nature, and walk in a new and holy life.

And if we sometimes, through weakness, fall into sin, we must not therefore despair of God's mercy, nor continue in sin, since Baptism is a seal and undoubted testimony that we have an *eternal* covenant of grace with God.

## I.

### TO INFANTS OF BELIEVERS.

And although our young children do not understand these things, we may not therefore exclude them from Baptism; for as they are, without their knowledge, partakers of the condemnation in Adam, so are they again received unto grace in Christ; as God speaketh unto Abraham, the father of all the faithful, and therefore unto us and our children, (Gen. 17 : 7,) saying: "I will establish my covenant between me and thee, and thy seed after thee, in their generations, for an everlasting covenant; to be a God unto thee, and to thy seed after thee." This also the Apostle Peter testifieth, with these words, (Acts 2 : 39:) "For the promise is unto you, and to your children, and to all that are afar off, even as many as the Lord our God shall call." Therefore God formerly commanded them to be circumcised, which was a seal of the Covenant, and of the righteousness of faith; and therefore Christ also embraced them, laid His hands upon them and blessed them. (Mark 10 : 16.)

Since then baptism is come in the place of circumcision, infants are to be baptized as heirs of the Kingdom of God and of His Covenant. And parents are in duty bound, further to instruct their children herein, when they shall arrive at years of discretion.

That therefore this holy ordinance of God may be administered to His glory, to our comfort, and to the edification of His Church, let us call upon His holy name.

## PRAYER.

O Almighty and eternal God, we beseech Thee that Thou wilt be pleased of Thine infinite mercy, graciously to look upon *these children*, and incorporate *them* by Thy Holy Spirit into Thy Son Jesus Christ, that *they* may be buried with Him into His death, and be raised with Him in newness of life; that *they* may daily follow Him, joyfully bearing *their* cross, and cleave unto Him in true faith, firm hope, and ardent love; that *they* may, with a comfortable sense of Thy favor, leave this life, which is nothing but a continual death; and at the last day, may appear without terror before the judgment-seat of Christ Thy Son, through Jesus Christ our Lord, who with Thee and the Holy Ghost, one only God, lives and reigns forever. AMEN.

### AN EXHORTATION TO THE PARENTS AND THOSE WHO COME WITH THEM TO BAPTISM.

Beloved in the Lord Jesus Christ, you have heard that baptism is an ordinance of God, to seal unto us and to our seed His covenant. Therefore it must be used for that end, and not out of custom or superstition. That it may then be manifest that you are thus minded, you are to answer sincerely to these questions:

*First.* Do you acknowledge, that although our children are conceived and born in sin, and therefore are subject to all miseries, yea, to condemnation itself; yet that they are sanctified\* in Christ, and therefore, as members of His Church, ought to be baptized?

---

\* *My children*, Ezek. 16 : 21. *They are holy*, 1 Cor. 7 : 14.

*Secondly.* Do you acknowledge the doctrine which is contained in the Old and New Testament, and in the articles of the Christian faith, and which is taught here in this Christian Church, to be the true and perfect* doctrine of salvation?

*Thirdly.* Do you promise and intend to see *these children*, when come to the years of discretion, instructed and brought up in the aforesaid doctrine, or to help or cause *them* to be instructed therein, to the utmost of your power?

*Answer.* Yes.

Then the Minister of God's Word in baptizing shall say:

————, I baptize thee, in the name of the Father, and of the Son, and of the Holy Ghost. AMEN.

### THANKSGIVING.

Almighty God and merciful Father, we thank and praise Thee, that Thou hast forgiven us, and our children, all our sins, through the blood of Thy beloved Son Jesus Christ, and received us through Thy Holy Spirit, as members of Thy only begotten Son, and adopted us to be Thy children, and sealed and confirmed the same unto us by holy baptism. We beseech Thee, through the same Son of Thy love, that Thou wilt be pleased always to govern *these* baptized *children* by Thy Holy Spirit; that *they* may be piously and religiously educated, increase and grow up in the Lord Jesus Christ; that *they* then may acknowledge Thy fatherly goodness and mercy, which Thou

---

* *Dutch:* Volkomene—complete.

hast shown to *them* and us; and live in all righteousness, under our only Teacher, King, and High-Priest, Jesus Christ; and manfully fight against and overcome sin, the devil and his whole dominion, to the end that *they* may eternally praise and magnify Thee, and Thy Son Jesus Christ, together with the Holy Ghost, the one only true God. AMEN.

Baptismal Chant.*

## II.

#### TO ADULT PERSONS.

However children of Christian parents, although they understand not this mystery, must be baptized by virtue of the Covenant; yet it is not lawful to baptize those who are come to years of discretion, except they first be sensible of their sins, and make confession both of their repentance and their faith in Christ. For this cause not only did John the Baptist preach, according to the command of God, the baptism of repentance, and baptize for the remission of sin, those who confessed their sins, (Mark 1 : 4 ;) but our Lord Jesus Christ also commanded His disciples to teach all nations, and then to baptize them, in the name of the Father, and of the Son, and of the Holy Ghost, adding this promise: "He that believeth and is baptized shall be saved." According to which rule the Apostles (Acts 2, 10, 16) baptized none who were of years of discretion, but such as made confession of their faith and repentance. Therefore it is not lawful now to baptize any other adult persons, than such as have been taught the mysteries of holy baptism by the

* See page 86.

preaching of the Gospel, and are able to give an account of their faith by the confession of the mouth.

Since therefore you, ―――――, are also desirous of holy baptism, to the end it may be to you a seal of your ingrafting into the Church of God ;* that it may appear that you do not only receive the Christian religion, in which you have been privately instructed by us, and of which also you have made confession before us, but that you, through the grace of God, intend and purpose to lead a life according to the same; you are sincerely to give answer before God and His Church:

*First.* Dost thou believe in the only true God, distinct in three persons, Father, Son, and Holy Ghost, who hath made heaven and earth, and all that in them is, of nothing, and still maintains and governs them, insomuch that nothing comes to pass, either in heaven or on earth, without His divine will?

*Answer.* Yes.

*Secondly.* Dost thou believe that thou art conceived and born in sin, and therefore art a child of wrath by nature, wholly incapable of doing any good and prone to all evil; and that thou hast frequently, both in thought, word, and deed, transgressed the commandments of the Lord; and art thou heartily sorry for these sins?

*Answer.* Yes.

*Thirdly.* Dost thou believe that Christ, who is the true and eternal God, and very man, who took His

---

* The remainder of this section, and the questions that follow, are used in this Church, in receiving to its fellowship those who enter it on confession of their faith in Christ.

human nature on Him out of the flesh and blood of the Virgin Mary, is given thee of God, to be thy Saviour; and that thou dost receive, by this faith, remission of sins in His blood; and that thou art made, by the power of the Holy Ghost, a member of Jesus Christ and of His Church?

*Answer.* Yes.

*Fourthly.* Dost thou assent to all the articles of the Christian religion, as they are taught here in this Christian Church, according to the Word of God; and purpose steadfastly to continue in the same doctrine to the end of thy life; and also dost thou reject all heresies and schisms, repugnant to this doctrine, and promise to persevere in the communion of our Christian Church, not only in the hearing of the Word, but also in the use of the Lord's Supper?

*Answer.* Yes.

*Fifthly.* Hast thou taken a firm resolution always to lead a Christian life; to forsake the world and its evil lusts, as is becoming the members of Christ and His Church; and to submit thyself to all Christian admonitions?

*Answer.* Yes.

The good and great God mercifully grant His grace and blessing to this thy purpose, through Jesus Christ. AMEN.

Then the Minister of God's Word, in baptizing shall say:

―――――, I baptize thee, in the name of the Father, and of the Son, and of the Holy Ghost. AMEN.

## The Office for the Administration of the Lord's Supper.

Beloved in the Lord Jesus Christ, attend to the words of the institution of the Holy Supper of our Lord Jesus Christ, as they are delivered by the holy Apostle Paul, 1 Cor. xi : 23–30.

"For I have received of the Lord that which also I delivered unto you, That the Lord Jesus, the same night in which he was betrayed, took bread; and when he had given thanks, he brake it, and said, Take, eat: this is my body, which is broken for you: this do in remembrance of me. After the same manner, also, he took the cup when he had supped, saying, This cup is the new testament in my blood: this do ye, as oft as ye drink it, in remembrance of me. For as often as ye eat this bread, and drink this cup, ye do show the Lord's death till he come. Wherefore, whosoever shall eat this bread, and drink this cup of the Lord unworthily, shall be guilty of the body and blood of the Lord. But let a man examine himself, and so let him eat of that bread and drink of that cup; for he that eateth and drinketh unworthily, eateth and drinketh damnation* to himself, not discerning the Lord's body."

That we may now celebrate the Supper of the Lord to our comfort, it is above all things necessary;

*First.* Rightly to examine ourselves.

*Secondly.* To direct the Supper to that end for

---

* *Greek :* Κριμα.  *Dutch :* Oordeel.  *English :* Judgment, condemnation.

which Christ hath ordained and instituted the same, namely, to His remembrance.

I. The true EXAMINATION of ourselves consists of these three parts:

*First.* That every one consider by himself his sins and the curse due to him for them, to the end that he may abhor and humble himself before God: considering that the wrath of God against sin is so great, that, rather than it should go unpunished, He hath punished the same in His beloved Son Jesus Christ, with the bitter and shameful death of the cross.

*Secondly.* That every one examine his own heart, whether he doth believe this faithful promise of God, that all his sins are forgiven him only for the sake of the passion and death of Jesus Christ; and that the perfect righteousness of Christ is imputed and freely given him as his own, yea, so perfectly as if he had satisfied in his own person for all his sins, and fulfilled all righteousness.

*Thirdly.* That every one examine his own conscience, whether he purposeth henceforth to show true thankfulness to God in his whole life, and to walk uprightly before Him; as also, whether he hath laid aside unfeignedly, all enmity, hatred, and envy, and doth firmly resolve henceforward to walk in true love and peace with his neighbor.

All those, then, who are thus disposed, God will certainly receive in mercy, and count them worthy partakers of the table of His Son Jesus Christ. On the contrary, those who do not feel this testimony in their hearts, eat and drink judgment to themselves. Therefore, we also, according to the command of

Christ and the Apostle Paul, admonish all those who are defiled with the following sins, to keep themselves from the table of the Lord, and declare to them that they have no part of the kingdom of Christ; such as all idolaters; all those who invoke deceased saints, angels, or other creatures; all those who worship images; all enchanters, diviners, charmers, and those who confide in such enchantments; all despisers of God and of His Word, and of the holy sacraments; all blasphemers; all those who are given to raise discord, sects, and mutiny, in church or state; all perjured persons; all those who are disobedient to their parents and superiors; all murderers, contentious persons, and those who live in hatred and envy against their neighbors; all adulterers, whoremongers, drunkards, thieves, usurers, robbers, gamesters, covetous; and all who lead offensive lives.

All these, while they continue in such sins, shall abstain from this meat, which Christ hath ordained only for the faithful, lest their judgment and condemnation be made the heavier.

But this is not designed, dearly beloved brethren and sisters in the Lord, to deject the contrite hearts of the faithful, as if none might come to the Supper of the Lord, but those who are without sin. For we do not come to this supper to testify thereby that we are perfect and righteous in ourselves; but on the contrary, considering that we seek our life out of ourselves, in Jesus Christ, we acknowledge that we lie in the midst of death. Therefore, notwithstanding we feel many infirmities and miseries in ourselves; as namely, that we have not perfect faith, and that we do not give ourselves to serve God with such zeal as we are bound, but have daily to strive with the weakness of our faith, and the evil lusts of our flesh; yet, since we are, by the grace of the Holy Ghost, sorry for these weaknesses, and earnestly desirous to fight against our unbelief, and to live according to all the commandments of God, therefore we rest assured that no sin or infirmity, which still remaineth, against our will, in us, can hinder us from being received of God in mercy, and from being made worthy partakers of this heavenly meat and drink.

II. Let us now also consider to what end the Lord hath instituted His Supper, namely, that we do it IN REMEMBRANCE OF HIM. Now, after this manner are we to remember Him by it.

1. That we be confidently persuaded in our hearts, that our Lord Jesus Christ, according to the promises made to our forefathers in the Old Testament, was sent of the Father into the world: that He assumed our flesh and blood: that He bore for us the wrath of God, under which we should have perished everlastingly, from the beginning of His incarnation to the end of His life upon earth: that He fulfilled for us all obedience to the divine law, and righteousness, especially when the weight of our sins and the wrath of God pressed out of Him the bloody sweat in the garden, where He was bound that we might be freed from our sins: that He afterward suffered innumerable reproaches, that we might never be confounded: that He, although innocent, was condemned to death, that we might be acquitted at the judgment-seat of God: yea, that He suffered His blessed body to be

nailed on the cross, that He might affix thereon the handwriting of our sins: that He also took upon Himself the curse due to us, that He might fill us with His blessings: that He humbled Himself unto the deepest reproach and pains of hell, both in body and soul, on the tree of the cross, when He cried out with a loud voice, *My God, My God! why hast thou forsaken me?* that we might be accepted of God, and never be forsaken of Him: and finally that He confirmed, with His death and shedding of His blood, the new and eternal testament, that covenant of grace and reconciliation, when He said, It is finished.

2. And, that we might firmly believe that we belong to this Covenant of Grace, the Lord Jesus Christ, in His last Supper, "took bread, and when He had given thanks, He brake it, and gave it to His disciples, and said, Take, eat, this is my body which is broken for you, this do in remembrance of me: in like manner also after supper, He took the cup, gave thanks and said, Drink ye all of it; this cup is the new testament in my blood, which is shed for you and for many, for the remission of sins; this do ye, as often as ye drink it, in remembrance of me." That is, as often as ye eat of this bread, and drink of this cup, you shall thereby, as by a sure remembrance and pledge, be admonished and assured of this my hearty love and faithfulness toward you: that whereas you should otherwise have suffered eternal death, I have given my body to the death of the cross, and shed my blood for you; and as certainly feed and nourish your hungry and thirsty soul with my crucified body and shed blood to everlasting life, as this

bread is broken before your eyes, and this cup is given to you, and you eat and drink the same with your mouth, in remembrance of me.

From this institution of the Holy Supper of our Lord Jesus Christ, we see that He directs our faith and trust to His perfect sacrifice, once offered on the cross, as to the only ground and foundation of our salvation; wherein He is become to our hungry and thirsty souls, the true meat and drink of life eternal. For by His death He hath taken away the cause of our eternal death and misery, namely, sin; and obtained for us the quickening Spirit, that we by the same, which dwelleth in Christ as the Head, and in us as His members, might have true communion with Him, and be made partakers of all His blessings, of life eternal, righteousness, and glory.

Besides, that we by the same Spirit may also be united as members of one Body in true brotherly love, as the holy Apostle saith, "For we, being many, are one bread and one body; for we are all partakers of that one bread." For as out of many grains one meal is ground and one bread baked, and out of many berries being pressed together, one wine floweth and mixeth itself together; so shall we all, who by a true faith are ingrafted into Christ, through brotherly love be altogether one body, for the sake of Christ, our beloved Saviour, who hath so exceedingly loved us; and shall show this, not only in word, but also in very deed towards one another.

Hereto assist us, the Almighty God and Father of

our Lord Jesus Christ, through His Holy Spirit. AMEN.

That we may obtain all this, let us humble ourselves before God, and with true faith implore His grace.

### PRAYER.

O Most merciful God and Father, we beseech Thee, that Thou wilt be pleased, in this Supper, in which we celebrate the glorious remembrance of the bitter death of Thy beloved Son Jesus Christ, to work in our hearts through the Holy Spirit, that we may daily, more and more, with true confidence, give ourselves up unto Thy Son Jesus Christ, so that our afflicted and contrite hearts, through the power of the Holy Ghost, may be fed and comforted with His true body and blood; yea, with Him, true God and man, that only heavenly bread : and that we may no longer live in our sins, but He in us, and we in Him, and thus truly be made partakers of the new and everlasting testament and covenant of grace : that we may not doubt that Thou wilt for ever be our gracious Father, never more imputing our sins unto us, and providing us, as thy beloved children and heirs, with all things necessary, as well for the body as the soul. Grant us also Thy grace, that we may take upon us our cross cheerfully, deny ourselves, confess our Saviour, and in all tribulations with uplifted heads expect our Lord Jesus Christ from heaven, where He will make our mortal bodies like unto His most glorious body, and take us unto Him in eternity. AMEN.

OUR FATHER, etc.

Strengthen us also by this Holy Supper in the Catholic undoubted Christian faith, whereof we make confession with our mouths and hearts, saying:

I BELIEVE IN GOD THE FATHER ALMIGHTY, MAKER OF HEAVEN AND EARTH;

AND IN JESUS CHRIST HIS ONLY SON OUR LORD; WHO WAS CONCEIVED BY THE HOLY GHOST, BORN OF THE VIRGIN MARY, SUFFERED UNDER PONTIUS PILATE, WAS CRUCIFIED, DEAD AND BURIED; HE DESCENDED INTO HELL; THE THIRD DAY HE ROSE AGAIN FROM THE DEAD; HE ASCENDED INTO HEAVEN; AND SITTETH ON THE RIGHT HAND OF GOD THE FATHER ALMIGHTY; FROM THENCE HE SHALL COME TO JUDGE THE QUICK AND THE DEAD.

I BELIEVE IN THE HOLY GHOST; THE HOLY CATHOLIC CHURCH; THE COMMUNION OF SAINTS; THE FORGIVENESS OF SINS; THE RESURRECTION OF THE BODY; AND THE LIFE EVERLASTING. AMEN.

That we may be now fed with the true heavenly bread, Christ Jesus, let us not cleave with our hearts unto the external bread and wine, but lift them up on high in heaven, where Christ Jesus is our advocate, at the right hand of His Heavenly Father, whither all the articles of our faith lead us; not doubting that through the working of the Holy Ghost, we shall as certainly be fed and refreshed in our souls with His body and blood, as we receive the holy bread and wine in remembrance of Him.

In breaking and distributing the bread the minister shall say:

The bread which we break, is the communion of the body of Christ.

And when he giveth the cup:

The cup of blessing, which we bless, is the communion of the blood of Christ.

During the communion, a Psalm shall or may be devoutly sung, or some chapter read, in remembrance of the death of Christ, as Isaiah liii, John xiii, xiv, xv, xvi, xvii, xviii, or the like.

---

After the communion, the minister shall say:

Beloved in the Lord, since the Lord hath now fed our souls at His table, let us therefore jointly praise His Holy name, with thanksgiving, and every one say in his heart, thus:

BLESS THE LORD, O MY SOUL; AND ALL THAT IS WITHIN ME, BLESS HIS HOLY NAME.

BLESS THE LORD, O MY SOUL; AND FORGET NOT ALL HIS BENEFITS.

WHO FORGIVETH ALL THINE INIQUITIES; WHO HEALETH ALL THY DISEASES.

WHO REDEEMETH THY LIFE FROM DESTRUCTION; WHO CROWNETH THEE WITH LOVING-KINDNESS AND TENDER MERCIES.

THE LORD IS MERCIFUL AND GRACIOUS; SLOW TO ANGER, AND PLENTEOUS IN MERCY.

HE HATH NOT DEALT WITH US AFTER OUR SINS; NOR REWARDED US ACCORDING TO OUR INIQUITIES.

FOR AS THE HEAVEN IS HIGH ABOVE THE EARTH;

SO GREAT IS HIS MERCY TOWARDS THEM THAT FEAR HIM.

AS FAR AS THE EAST IS FROM THE WEST; SO FAR HATH HE REMOVED OUR TRANSGRESSIONS FROM US.

LIKE AS A FATHER PITIETH HIS CHILDREN; SO THE LORD PITIETH THEM THAT FEAR HIM.

WHO HATH NOT SPARED HIS OWN SON, BUT DELIVERED HIM UP FOR US ALL, AND GIVEN US ALL THINGS WITH HIM. THEREFORE GOD COMMENDETH THEREWITH HIS LOVE TOWARDS US, IN THAT WHILE WE WERE YET SINNERS, CHRIST DIED FOR US; MUCH MORE THEN, BEING NOW JUSTIFIED BY HIS BLOOD, WE SHALL BE SAVED FROM WRATH THROUGH HIM. FOR, IF WHEN WE WERE ENEMIES, WE WERE RECONCILED TO GOD BY THE DEATH OF HIS SON; MUCH MORE BEING RECONCILED, WE SHALL BE SAVED BY HIS LIFE. THEREFORE SHALL MY MOUTH AND HEART SHOW FORTH THE PRAISE OF THE LORD FROM THIS TIME FORTH FOR EVERMORE. AMEN.

**Let every one say with an attentive heart:**

O Almighty, merciful God and Father, we render Thee most humble and hearty thanks, that Thou hast, of Thine infinite mercy, given us Thine only begotten Son, for a mediator and a sacrifice for our sins, and to be our meat and drink unto life eternal; and that Thou givest us lively faith, whereby we are made partakers of these Thy benefits. Thou hast also been pleased, that Thy beloved Son Jesus Christ should institute and ordain His Holy Supper for the confirmation of the same. Grant, we beseech Thee, O faithful God and Father, that through the operation of Thy Holy Spirit, the commemoration of the death of our Lord Jesus Christ may tend to the daily increase of our faith, and of our saving fellowship with Him: Through Jesus Christ Thy Son, in whose Name we conclude our prayers, saying:

OUR FATHER, etc.

# Office

#### for

## The Confirmation of Marriage.

---

God be merciful unto us, and bless us, and cause His face to shine upon us, through Jesus Christ our Lord. Amen.

**Then the Minister shall say to all present:**

In the name of Almighty God, I demand of each person here present, that if they know any good reason why this man and this woman should not be joined in Marriage, they do now declare the same as they shall answer to the Searcher of hearts.

**And to the man and woman:**

I charge you both, before God and the Lord Jesus Christ, who shall judge the quick and the dead at His appearing and His kingdom, that if either of you know any reason why ye may not lawfully be joined together in Marriage ye do now declare it,

*Then the Minister shall say to all present:*

Marriage, ordained of God in Eden, was confirmed at the wedding in Cana of Galilee by the gracious presence, and the first miracle of our divine Lord Jesus Christ, who hath also said, What God hath joined together let not man put asunder. Moreover, His holy Apostle St. Paul hath commended unto the husband the example of Christ in loving His Church, and unto the wife the willing subjection of the Church unto Christ as her head. Whence we learn that Marriage is well pleasing to God our Saviour, and most honorable to all who live worthily therein.

*And to the man and woman:*

You who are the bridegroom are to remember that God hath set you to be the head of your wife, that you, according to your ability, may guide her with discretion. You are to cherish her as your own body, to sustain, honor, and defend her, in joy and in sorrow, in sickness and in health.

You who are the bride, are to honor your husband as the head of the household according to the word of God; to love and to cherish him in joy and in sorrow, in sickness and in health; that you may be truly a help meet for him in all the duties, trials, and changes of this mortal life.

Wherefore, you, ―――, and you, ―――, having now understood that God hath instituted Marriage, and what He commands you therein, are you willing thus to behave yourselves in this holy estate, and are you desirous that you be confirmed in the same?

*Answer.* YES.

And the Minister shall say:

### LET US PRAY.

O most holy and most merciful Lord God! we beseech Thee for these Thy servant and handmaid, that they may, with a reverent trust in Thee, enter into the Covenant of Marriage, as they now propose, and truly keep all the vows which they are about to make according to Thy word. Grant this, O Father, with the forgiveness of our sins, through Christ Thy Son. AMEN.

---

Then the Minister shall bid the man and the woman join their right hands; which being done, he shall say to the man:

Dost thou, _____, take this woman, _____, before God and these witnesses, to be thy wife?

Answer. YES.

Dost thou promise to love her faithfully; never to forsake her; to maintain and defend her; to live holily with her; and to keep faith and truth to her in all things according to the holy Gospel?

Answer. YES.

The Minister shall then say to the woman:

Dost thou, _____, take this man, _____, before God and these witnesses, to be thy husband?

Answer. YES.

Dost thou promise to love him faithfully; never to forsake him; to be obedient to him; to live holily with him; and to keep faith and truth to him in all things according to the holy Gospel?

Answer. YES.

[Then the Minister shall say to the man:

What pledge dost thou give that thou wilt perform these thy vows ?

The man shows the ring.

Then the man (the Minister guiding his hand) shall place the ring on the fourth finger of her left hand.

And the man shall say:

*Eliz. V.* ——, I give this ring to thee, in pledge of the union between thee and me, which nothing but death shall break.

And the woman shall say:

*Wallace* ——, I take this ring from thee, in pledge of the union between thee and me, which nothing but death shall break.]

Then the Minister shall bid the married persons to kneel down, and shall exhort the congregation to pray for them.

### LET US PRAY.

O God! our heavenly Father, Thou hast heard these promises of Thy servant and handmaid to each other; mercifully condescend to unite their hearts and lives by all the grace and true affection of a happy Marriage. May their love never know change, nor doubt, nor decay. May they be blessed in the knowledge of Christ Thy Son; blessed in each other—the husband in the wife, the wife in the husband; blessed in their home, in their basket and in their store, in their trials and in their comforts; blessed in life, blessed in death, and blessed in eternity, through Jesus Christ our Lord and only Saviour, who hath taught us to pray,

OUR FATHER, etc.

Then the Minister, taking their clasped hands in his, will say:

Listen now! Since you _Wallace_ and you _Elsy_ have consented together after God's holy ordinance of Marriage, and have plighted your faith and truth to each other in the presence of God and these witnesses, [and have confirmed the same by giving and receiving a ring;] now, therefore,

In the name of the Father, and of the Son, and of the Holy Ghost, I pronounce you husband and wife! Whom therefore God Almighty hath joined together let not man put asunder.

The Lord bless you and keep you!

The Lord make His face shine upon you, and be gracious unto you!

The Lord lift up His countenance upon you, and give you peace! AMEN.

# Office

### for

# The Burial of the Dead.

### I.

When a brief prefatory service at the house, before going to the church, is desired, the portion of Holy Scripture from St. John's Gospel, on page 43, may be used, together with the prayer for that purpose on page 46.
And on entering the church, the Minister may use the following sentences.
Or, if all the services be performed at the house, he may begin with these sentences.

Enter not into judgment with thy servant: for in thy sight shall no man living be justified.

Thou turnest man to destruction; and sayest, Return, ye children of men.

By one man sin entered into the world, and death by sin, and so death hath passed upon all men, because that all have sinned.

We brought nothing into *this* world, *and it is* certain we can carry nothing out.

*As for* man, his days *are* as grass: as a flower of the field, so he flourisheth. For the wind passeth over it, and it is gone; and the place thereof shall know it no more.

We are strangers before Thee and sojourners, as were all our fathers: our days on the earth are as a shadow, and there is none abiding.

II.

Then the Minister will say:

Hear the word of God as it is written in the fourteenth chapter of the Book of Job.

Man *that is* born of a woman *is* of few days, and full of trouble. He cometh forth like a flower, and is cut down: he fleeth also as a shadow, and continueth not. And dost Thou open Thine eyes upon such an one, and bringest me into judgment with Thee? Who can bring a clean *thing* out of an unclean? not one. Seeing his days *are* determined, the number of his months *are* with Thee, Thou hast appointed his bounds that he cannot pass; Turn from him, that he may rest, till he shall accomplish, as an hireling, his day. For there is hope of a tree, if it be cut down, that it will sprout again, and that the tender branch thereof will not cease. Though the root thereof wax old in the earth, and the stock thereof die in the ground; *Yet* through the scent of water it will bud, and bring forth boughs like a plant. But man dieth, and wasteth away: yea, man giveth up the ghost, and where *is* he? *As* the waters fail from the sea, and the flood decayeth and drieth up: So man lieth down, and riseth not: till the heavens *be* no more, they shall not awake, nor be raised out of their sleep. O that Thou wouldst hide me in the grave, that Thou wouldest keep me secret, until Thy wrath be past, that Thou wouldest appoint me a set time, and remember me! If a man die, shall he live *again?* all the days of my appointed time will I wait, till my change come. Thou shalt call, and I will answer Thee: Thou wilt have a desire to the work of Thine hands.

<small>Hear the comfortable words of the Gospel of our Saviour Jesus Christ, as they are written in the eleventh chapter of St. John:</small>

Then said Martha unto Jesus, Lord, if Thou hadst been here, my brother had not died. But I know that, even now, whatsoever Thou wilt ask of God, God will give it Thee. Jesus sáith unto her, Thy brother shall rise again. Martha saith unto him, I know that he shall rise again in the resurrection at the last day. Jesus said unto her, I am the Resurrection and the Life: he that believeth in me, though he were dead, yet shall he live: and whosoever liveth and believeth in me shall never die. Believest thou this? She saith unto him, Yea, Lord: I believe that Thou art the Christ, the Son of God, which should come into the world.

<small>Hear the word of God as it is written in the fifteenth chapter of St. Paul's first Epistle to the Corinthians, beginning with the thirty-fifth verse:</small>

But some *man* will say, How are the dead raised up? and with what body do they come? *Thou* fool, that which thou sowest is not quickened except it die: And that which thou sowest, thou sowest not that body that shall be, but bare grain; it may chance of wheat, or of some other *grain:* But God giveth it a body as it hath pleased Him, and to every seed his own body. All flesh *is* not the same flesh; but *there is* one *kind of* flesh of men, another flesh of beasts, another of fishes, *and* another of birds. *There are* also celestial bodies, and bodies terrestrial: but the glory of the celestial *is* one, and the *glory* of the terrestrial *is* another. *There is* one glory of the sun, and another glory of the moon, and another glory of the stars; for *one* star differeth from *another* star in glory. So also *is* the resurrection of the dead. It is sown in corruption, it is raised in incorruption: It is sown in dishonor, it is raised in glory: it is sown in weakness, it is raised in power: It is sown a natural body, it is raised a spiritual body. There is a natural body, and there is a spiritual body. And so it is written, The first man Adam was made a living soul, the last Adam *was made* a quickening spirit. Howbeit, that *was* not first which is spiritual, but that which is natural; and afterward that which is spiritual. The first man *is* of the earth, earthy: the second man *is* the Lord from heaven. As *is* the earthy, such *are* they also that are earthy: and as *is* the heavenly, such *are* they also that are heavenly. And as we have borne the image of the earthy, we shall also bear the image of the heavenly. Now this I say, brethren, that flesh and blood cannot inherit the kingdom of God; neither doth corruption inherit incorruption. Behold, I show you a mystery; We shall not all sleep, but we shall all be changed, in a moment, in the twinkling of an eye, at the last trump: for the trumpet shall sound, and the dead shall be raised incorruptible, and we shall be changed.

For this corruptible must put on incorruption, and this mortal *must* put on immortality. So when this corruptible shall have put on incorruption, and this mortal shall have put on immortality, then shall be brought to pass the saying that is written, Death is swallowed up in victory. O death, where *is* thy sting? O grave, where *is* thy victory? The sting of death *is* sin; and the strength of sin *is* the law. But thanks *be* to God, which giveth us the victory, through our Lord Jesus Christ. Therefore, my beloved brethren, be ye steadfast, unmovable, always abounding in the work of the Lord, forasmuch as ye know that your labor is not in vain in the Lord.

## III.

### [FOR A CHILD.]

[Hear the Gospel of our Saviour Jesus Christ, in reference to little children.

And they brought young children to Him, that he should touch them; and His disciples rebuked those that brought them. But when Jesus saw it He was much displeased, and said unto them, Suffer the little children to come unto me, and forbid them not, for of such is the kingdom of heaven. Verily, I say unto you, whosoever shall not receive the kingdom of heaven as a little child, he shall not enter therein.

Take heed that ye despise not one of these little ones; for I say unto you, that in heaven their angels do always behold the face of my Father which is in heaven.

For the Son of Man is come to save that which was lost. How think ye? If a man have a hundred sheep, and one of them be gone astray, doth he not leave the ninety and nine and goeth into the mountains and seeketh that which is gone astray? And if so be that he find it, verily I say unto you, he rejoiceth more of that sheep than of the ninety and nine which went not astray. Even so it is not the will of your Father which is in heaven, that one of these little ones should perish.

The Lord gave and the Lord hath taken away. Blessed be the name of the Lord.]

[PRAYER TO BE SAID AT THE HOUSE.

O God, merciful God, Father of our Lord Jesus Christ, who hast said, Blessed are they that mourn, for they shall be comforted; under the shadow of Thy judgments we come to Thee and acknowledge Thee to be the Lord alone. Thou hast entered this house with Thy chastenings; oh! be Thou nigh in Thy tender compassion to these afflicted ones. Bless Thy sorrowing servants with Thy consolations, which are neither few nor small.

Convert them wholly to Thyself, and fill their bleeding hearts with Thy love. Make the night of their grief to be light by Thy grace.

Deliver us Thy servants, we pray Thee, from the bondage of our sins, that we may be free from the fear of death, and be ready at Thy coming. Yea, Lord, for Christ's sake, sanctify us by Thy Holy Spirit, that whether we live, we may live unto the Lord, or whether we die, we may die unto the Lord; whether we live or die, we may be the Lord's. AMEN.]

## IV.

### [ADDRESS]

#### PRAYER.

Eternal, merciful God and Father, the eternal salvation of the living and the everlasting life of the dying, seeing that Thou hast death and life in Thy hand alone, we beseech Thee, grant us the grace of Thy Holy Spirit, to teach us rightly to acknowledge our misery, and patiently to bear Thy chastenings. We know that they are not the evidences of Thy wrath, but of Thy fatherly love towards us, that we should not be condemned with the world. O Lord, increase our faith in Thine infinite mercy, that we may be more and more united to Christ, as members to their spiritual head, to whom Thou wilt make us conform in sufferings and in glory. Lighten the cross, so that our weakness may be able to bear it. Grant us to experience the blessed comfort of the remission of sins, through Christ, that we by that shield may overcome all the assaults of Satan. May His innocent blood wash away all the stain and uncleanness of our sins, and His righteousness answer for our unrighteousness in Thy last judgment. Arm us with faith and hope, that we may not be ashamed nor confounded by the terror of death; but when our bodily eyes are closing in darkness, may the eyes of our souls be directed towards thee. O Lord, we commit our souls into Thy hands; forsake us, not in our last extremity, and that only for the sake of Jesus Christ, who taught us to pray—OUR FATHER, etc.

## V.

*Then standing near the coffin, or having reached the place of burial, the Minister will say:*

In the midst of life we are in death!
What helper shall we seek but Thee, O Lord,
Who because of our sins art justly angry!
O holy God! O holy and strong, holy and compassionate Saviour,
Give us not over to bitter death!

*Then, while the earth shall be cast upon the body by some standing by, the Minister will say:*

Forasmuch as it hath pleased Almighty God to take out of this world the soul of our departed *brother*, we therefore commit *his* body to the ground; earth to earth, ashes to ashes, dust to dust; looking for the general Resurrection in the last day, and the life of the world to come, through our Lord Jesus Christ; at whose second coming in glorious majesty to judge the world, the earth and the sea shall give up their dead; and the corruptible bodies of those who sleep in Him shall be changed, and made like unto His own glorious body; according to the mighty working whereby He is able to subdue all things unto Himself.

I know that my Redeemer liveth, and that He shall stand at the latter day upon the earth. And though after my skin worms destroy this body, yet in my flesh shall I see God, whom I shall see for myself, and mine eyes shall behold, and not another.

PRAYER.

O God, whose days are without end, and whose mercies cannot be numbered: make us, we beseech Thee, deeply sensible of the shortness and uncertainty of human life; and let Thy Holy Spirit lead us through this vale of misery, in holiness and righteousness all the days of our lives: that when we shall have served Thee in our generation, we may be gathered unto our fathers, having the testimony of a good conscience; in the communion of the Christian Church; in the confidence of a certain faith; in the comfort of a reasonable, religious, and holy hope; in favor with Thee our God, and in perfect charity with the world: all which we ask through Jesus Christ our Lord. AMEN.

Almighty God, our heavenly Father, who, in Thy perfect wisdom and mercy, hast ended for Thy servants departed the voyage of this troublous life; Grant, we beseech Thee, that we who are still to continue our course amidst earthly dangers, temptations, and troubles, may evermore be protected by Thy mercy; and finally come to the haven of eternal salvation through Jesus Christ our Lord. AMEN.

The grace of our Lord Jesus Christ, and the love of God, and the fellowship of the Holy Ghost, be with us all evermore. AMEN.

# Form

FOR

## Ordaining Elders and Deacons,

### WHEN ORDAINED AT THE SAME TIME.

If ordained separately, this form shall be used as occasion requires.

Beloved Christians, you know that we have several times published unto you the names of our brethren here present, who are chosen to the office of Elders and Deacons in this Church, to the end that we might know whether any person had aught to allege, why they should not be ordained in their respective offices. And whereas no one hath appeared before us, who hath alleged any thing lawful against them, we shall therefore at present, in the name of the Lord, proceed to their ordination.

But first, you, who are to be ordained, and all those who are here present, shall attend to a short declaration from the Word of God concerning the institution and the office of Elders and Deacons.

Of the Elders, it is to be observed that the word elder or eldest, which is taken out of the Old Testament, and signifieth a person who is placed in an honorable office of government over others, is applied to two sorts of persons who administer in the Church of Jesus Christ: for the Apostle saith, "The elders that rule well shall be counted worthy of double honor, especially they who labor in the word and doctrine." Hence it is evident that there were two sorts of elders in the Apostolic Church; the former whereof did labor in the word and doctrine, and the latter did not. The first were the Ministers of the Word and Pastors, who preached the Gospel and administered the Sacraments; but the others, who did not labor in the Word, and still did serve in the Church, bore a particular office, namely, that they had the oversight of the Church, and ruled the same with the Ministers of the Word. For Paul (Rom. xii: 8) having spoken of the ministry of the Word, and also of the office of distribution or Deaconship, speaketh, afterwards particularly of this office, saying, "He that ruleth, let him do it with diligence;" likewise, in another place, (1 Cor. xii : 28,) he counts "governments" among the gifts and offices which God hath instituted in the Church. Thus we see that these sorts of ministers are added to the others who preach the Gospel, to aid and assist them, as in the Old Testament the common Levites were to the priests in the service of the tabernacle, in things which they could not perform alone; notwithstanding, the offices always remained distinct one from the other.

Moreover, it is proper that such men should be joined to the Ministers of the Word in the government of the Church, that thereby all tyranny and lording may be kept out of the Church of God, which may sooner creep in when the government is placed in the hands of one alone, or of a very few. And thus the Ministers of the Word, together with the Elders, form a body or assembly, being as a council of the Church, representing the whole Church, to which Christ alludes when he saith: " Tell the Church;" which can in no wise be understood of all and every member of the Church in particular, but very properly of those who govern the Church, out of which they are chosen. )

Therefore, in the *first* place, the office of the Elders is, together with the Ministers of the Word, to take the oversight of the Church, which is committed to them, and diligently to look whether every one properly deports himself in his confession and conversation; to admonish those who behave themselves disorderly; and to prevent as much as possible, the Sacraments from being profaned; also to act, according to the Christian discipline against the impenitent, and to receive the penitent again into the bosom of the Church: as it doth appear, not only from the above-mentioned saying of Christ, but also from many other places of holy writ, (as 1 Cor. v. and 2 Cor. ii.,) that these things are not alone intrusted to one or two persons, but to many who are ordained thereto.

*Secondly.* Since the Apostle enjoineth, that all things shall be done decently and in order, amongst Christians, and that no other persons ought to serve in the Church of Christ but those who are lawfully called, according to the Christian ordinance; therefore it is also the duty of the Elders to pay regard to it, and in all occurrences which relate to the welfare and good order of the Church, to be assistant with their good counsel and advice to the Ministers of the Word, yea, also to serve all Christians with advice and consolation.

*Thirdly.* It is also their duty particularly to have regard unto the doctrine and conversation of the Ministers of the Word, to the end that all things may be directed to the edification of the Church; and that no strange doctrine be taught, according to that which we read, (Acts xx.,) where the Apostle exhorteth to watch diligently against the wolves which might come into the sheepfold of Christ; for the performance of which the Elders are in duty bound diligently to search the Word of God, and continually to be meditating on the mysteries of faith.

Concerning the DEACONS; of the origin and institution of their office we may read in the sixth chapter of the Acts of the Apostles, where we find that the Apostles themselves did in the beginning serve the poor, "At whose feet was brought the price of the things that were sold: and distribution was made unto every man according as he had need. But afterwards, when a murmuring arose, because the widows of the Grecians were neglected in the daily ministration," men were chosen, by the advice of the Apostles, who should make the service of the poor their peculiar business, to the end that the Apostles might continually give themselves to prayer, and to the Ministry of the Word. And this has been continued from that time forward in the Church, as appears from the Epistle to the Romans, (xii : 8,) where the Apostle, speaking of this office, saith, "He that giveth, let him do it with simplicity." And in first Corinthians, (xii : 28,) speaking of "helps," he means those who are appointed in the Church to help and assist the poor and indigent in time of need.

From which passages we may easily gather what the Deacons' office is, namely: That they, in the *first* place, collect and preserve with greatest fidelity and diligence the alms and goods which are given to the poor: yea, to use their utmost endeavors, that many good means be procured for the relief of the poor.

The *second* part of their office consists in distribution, wherein are required not only discretion and prudence, to bestow the alms only on objects of charity, but also cheerfulness and simplicity, to assist the poor with compassion and hearty affection; as the Apostle requires. (Rom xii. and 2 Cor. ix.) For which end it is very beneficial, that they administer relief to the poor and indigent, not only with external gifts, but also with comfortable words from Scripture.

To the end, therefore, beloved brethren, ———, that every one may hear that you are willing to take your respective offices upon you, ye shall answer to the following questions:

And in the first place I ask you, both Elders and Deacons, whether ye do not feel in your hearts, that ye are lawfully called of God's Church, and consequently of God himself, to these your respective holy offices?

*Secondly.* Whether ye believe the books of the Old and New Testament to be the only word of God, and the perfect doctrine of salvation, and do reject all doctrines repugnant thereto?

*Thirdly.* Whether ye promise, agreeably to said doctrine, faithfully, according to your ability, to discharge your respective offices, as they are here described : ye Elders in the government of the Church together with the Ministers of the word : and ye Deacons in the ministration to the poor ? Do ye also jointly promise to walk in all godliness, and to submit yourselves, in case ye should become remiss in your duty, to the admonitions of the Church ?

Upon which they shall answer, *Yes.*

Then the Minister shall say :

The Almighty God and Father replenish you all with His grace, that ye may faithfully and fruitfully discharge your respective offices. AMEN.

The Minister shall further exhort them, and the whole congregation, in the following manner :

Therefore, ye Elders, be diligent in the government of the Church which is committed to you, and the Ministers of the word. Be also, as watchmen over the house and city of God, faithful to admonish and to caution every one against his ruin. Take heed, that purity of doctrine and godliness of life be maintained in the Church of God. And, ye Deacons, be diligent in collecting the alms, prudent and cheerful in the distribution of the same : assist the oppressed, provide for the true widows and orphans, show liberality unto all men, but especially to the household of faith.

Be ye all with one accord faithful in your offices, and *hold the mystery of the faith in a pure conscience,* being good examples unto all the people. In so doing you will *purchase to yourselves a good degree, and great boldness in the faith which is in Christ Jesus, and hereafter enter into the joy of your Lord.* On the other hand, beloved Christians, receive these men as servants of God: count the Elders that rule well worthy of double honor, give yourselves willingly to their inspection and government. Provide the Deacons with good means to assist the indigent. Be charitable; ye rich, give liberally, and contribute willingly. And, ye poor, be poor in spirit, and deport yourselves respectfully toward your benefactors; be thankful to them and avoid murmuring: follow Christ, for the food of your souls, but not for bread. "Let him that stole," or who hath been burthensome to his neighbor, "steal no more: but rather let him labor, working with his hands the things which are good, that he may give to him that needeth." Each of you, doing these things in your respective callings, shall receive of the Lord *the reward of righteousness.* But since we are unable of ourselves, let us call upon the name of the Lord, saying:

PRAYER.

O Lord God and heavenly Father, we thank Thee that it hath pleased Thee, for the better edification of Thy Church, to ordain in it, besides the Ministers of the word, rulers, and assistants, by whom Thy Church may be preserved in peace and prosperity, and the indigent assisted; and that Thou hast at present granted us in this place, men who are of good testimony, and we hope endowed with Thy spirit. We beseech Thee, replenish them more and more with such gifts as are necessary for them in their ministration; with the gifts of wisdom, courage, discretion, and benevolence, to the end that every one may, in his respective office, acquit himself as is becoming; the Elders in taking diligent heed unto the doctrine and conversation, in keeping out the wolves from the sheep-fold of Thy beloved Son, and in admonishing and reproving disorderly persons. In like manner, the Deacons in carefully receiving, and liberally and prudently distributing of the alms to the poor, and in comforting them with Thy holy word. Give grace both to the Elders and Deacons, that they may persevere in their faithful labor, and never become weary by reason of any trouble, pain, or persecution of the world. Grant also, especially, Thy divine grace to this people, over whom they are placed, that they may willingly submit themselves to the good exhortation of the Elders, counting them worthy of honor for their work's sake; give also unto the rich liberal hearts toward the poor, and to the poor grateful hearts toward those who help and serve them; to the end that every one acquitting himself of his duty, Thy holy name may thereby be magnified, and the kingdom of Thy Son Jesus Christ enlarged, in whose name we conclude our prayers,

OUR FATHER, etc.

# Sentences

(Which may be read during the collection of alms.)

### I.

Honor the Lord with thy substance, and with the first-fruits of all thine increase: So shall thy barns be filled with plenty, and thy presses shall burst out with new wine. Prov. iii : 9, 10.

### II.

Blessed *is* he that considereth the poor: the Lord will deliver him in time of trouble. Psalm xli : 1.

### III.

But this *I say*, He which soweth sparingly shall reap also sparingly ; and he which soweth bountifully shall reap also bountifully.

Every man according as he purposeth in his heart, *so let him give ;* not grudgingly, or of necessity: for God loveth a cheerful giver. 2 Cor. ix : 6, 7.

### IV.

Cast thy bread upon the waters: for thou shalt find it after many days. Eccles. xi : 1.

### V.

For ye know the grace of our Lord Jesus Christ, that, though He was rich, yet for your sakes He became poor, that ye through His poverty might be rich. 2 Cor. viii : 9.

### VI.

I have showed you all things, how that so laboring ye ought to support the weak, and to remember the words of the Lord Jesus, how He said, It is more blessed to give than to receive. Acts xx : 35.

### VII.

In the morning sow thy seed, and in the evening withhold not thine hand: for thou knowest not whether shall prosper, either this or that, or whether they both *shall be* alike good. Eccles. xi : 6.

### VIII.

And let us not be weary in well-doing : for in due season we shall reap if we faint not. Gal. vi : 9.

### IX.

And the King shall answer and say unto them, Verily I say unto you, Inasmuch as ye have done *it* unto one of the least of these my brethren, ye have done *it* unto me. Matt. xxv : 40.

### X.

There is that scattereth, and yet increaseth; and *there is* that withholdeth more than is meet, but it *tendeth* to poverty.

The liberal soul shall be made fat: and he that watereth shall be watered also himself. Prov. xi : 24, 25.

## XI.

Thanks *be* unto God for His unspeakable gift. 2 Cor. ix : 15.

## XII.

For if there be first a willing mind, *it is* accepted according to that a man hath, *and* not according to that he hath not. 2 Cor. viii : 12.

# Christian Prayers.

## A Confession of Sin.

*From the Liturgy of the Reformed Dutch Church.*

O Eternal God, and most merciful Father, we humbly prostrate ourselves before Thy high majesty, against which we have so often and grievously offended, and acknowledge, if Thou shouldst enter into judgment with us, that we have deserved nothing but eternal death. For besides that we all are by original sin unclean in Thy sight and children of wrath, conceived in sin and brought forth in iniquity, whereby all manner of evil lusts, striving against Thee and our neighbor, dwell within us; we have also, indeed, frequently and without end, transgressed Thy precepts, neglected what Thou hast commanded us, and done what Thou hast expressly forbidden us. We have strayed like sheep, and have greatly offended against Thee, which we acknowledge, and are heartily sorry for; nay, we confess to our shame, and to the praise of Thy mercy towards us, that our sins are more than the hairs of our head, and that we are indebted ten thousand talents, but not able to pay.

Wherefore we are not worthy to be called Thy children; nor to lift up our eyes towards heaven, to pour out our prayers before Thee. Nevertheless, O Lord God, and merciful Father, knowing that Thou dost not desire the death of a sinner, but that he may turn from his wickedness and live; and that Thy mercy is infinite, which Thou showest unto those who return to Thee; we heartily call upon Thee, trusting in our Mediator Jesus Christ, who is that Lamb of God that taketh away the sins of the world; and we beseech thee to commiserate our infirmity, forgiving us all our sins for Christ's sake. Wash us in the pure fountain of His blood, that we may become clean and white as snow. Cover our nakedness with His innocence and righteousness, for the glory of Thy name's sake; clear our understanding of all blindness, and our hearts of all hardness and pride; write Thy laws (according to Thy promise) in the tables of our hearts, and strengthen us to delight and walk in the same, to the praise and glory of Thy name, and to the edification of Thy Church. O gracious Father, we ask for, and desire all these things in the name of Jesus Christ, who hath taught us thus to pray—OUR FATHER, etc.

# The Litany.*

**From the Provisional Liturgy of the Reformed Dutch Church.**

O GOD the Father of Heaven, have mercy upon us.

O God the Son, Redeemer of the world, have mercy upon us.

O God the Holy Ghost, have mercy upon us.

Be merciful unto us, and spare us, O Lord.

Be merciful unto us, and deliver us, O Lord.

From all sin, from all error, from all evil, from the wiles of the devil, deliver us, O Lord.

From dying suddenly and unprepared; from pestilence and famine, from war and slaughter, from sedition and conspiracy, from lightning and tempest, from everlasting death, deliver us, O Lord.

By the mystery of Thy holy Incarnation, by Thy holy Nativity, by Thy Baptism, Fasting, and Temptations, deliver us, O Lord.

By Thine Agony and bloody Sweat, by Thy Cross and Passion, by Thy Death and Burial, by Thy Resurrection and Ascension, by the coming of the Holy Ghost the Comforter, deliver us, O Lord.

In all time of our tribulation, in all time of our felicity, in the hour of death, in the day of judgment, deliver us, O Lord.

---

\* This is a literal translation from the Reformer Bucer's "Reformation of Doctrine and Worship."

We sinners beseech Thee to hear us:

That it may please Thee to rule and govern Thy holy Church Universal.

That it may please Thee to preserve in soundness of word and holiness of life, all pastors and ministers of Thy Church.

That it may please Thee to remove all sects and scandals.

That it may please Thee to bring back into the way of truth all such as wander and have been led astray.

That it may please Thee to crush Satan under our feet.

That it may please Thee to send forth faithful laborers into Thy harvest.

That it may please Thee to grant the increase of Thy Word and the fruit of Thy Spirit unto all that hear.

That it may please Thee to raise the fallen, and strengthen those that stand.

That it may please Thee to console the weak-hearted, and succor the tempted.

That it may please Thee to give peace and concord unto all rulers and governors.

That it may please Thee to guide and protect our chief magistrate, with all his counsellors.

That it may please Thee to bless and preserve our people, and all in authority among us.

That it may please Thee to look upon the afflicted, and those that are in danger; and to comfort them.

That it may please Thee to succor all women in the perils of child-birth.

That it may please Thee to cherish and protect young children, and sick persons.

That it may please Thee to defend and suitably provide for the orphans and widows.

That it may please Thee to grant freedom unto captives.

That it may please Thee to have mercy upon all men.

That it may please Thee to forgive our enemies, persecutors, and slanderers, and to convert them.

That it may please Thee to give and preserve the fruits of the earth.

That it may please Thee to grant all these our requests.

We beseech Thee to hear us.

Lamb of God, who takest away the sins of the world, have mercy upon us.

Lamb of God, who takest away the sins of the world, grant us Thy peace.

Lord, deal not with us according to our sins, neither reward us according to our iniquities.

O God, Merciful Father, who despisest not the groans of the contrite, nor rejectest the desire of the sorrowful : be favorable to our prayers, which, in our afflictions that continually oppress us, we pour out before Thee ; and graciously hear them ; that those things which the craft of the devil or of man worketh against us, may be brought to naught, and by the counsel of Thy goodness be scattered ; that being hurt by no persecutions, we may ever give thanks unto Thee in Thy holy Church ; through Jesus Christ our Lord.

O God, from whom all holy desires, all good counsels, and all just works proceed: give unto Thy servants that peace which the world cannot give; that both our hearts may be set to obey Thy commandments, and also that we, being defended from the fear of our enemies, may, by Thy protection, pass our time in rest and quietness: through Jesus Christ our Lord. AMEN.

# Prayers

Selected or abbreviated from the Liturgy of the Reformed Dutch Church.

(Which may be used after sermon at the discretion of the Minister.)

O HEAVENLY Father, Thy word is perfect, converting the soul; a sure testimony, making wise the simple, enlightening the eyes of the blind; and a powerful means unto salvation for all those who believe. And whereas we are not only blind by nature, but even incapable of doing any good; and also since Thou wilt help none but those who are of a broken and contrite heart; we beseech Thee to enlighten our understanding with Thy Holy Spirit, and give us a meek heart, free from all haughtiness and carnal knowledge, that we, hearing Thy word, may rightly understand it, and regulate our life accordingly. Be graciously pleased to convert all those who still stray from Thy truth, that we, together with them, may serve Thee in true holiness and righteousness all the days of our life. We crave all these things for Christ's sake. AMEN.

HAVE compassion on us, O most bounteous God and Father, and forgive us all our sins for that holy passion of Thy well-beloved Son Jesus Christ. Grant us also the grace of Thy Holy Spirit, that we may, with all our hearts, study to know our own unrighteousness and sincerely abhor ourselves; that sin may be mortified in us and we may be raised up to a new life; that we may bring forth genuine fruits of holiness and righteousness, which through Christ Jesus are acceptable to Thee. Give us to understand Thy holy word according to Thy Divine will, that we may learn thereby to put our whole trust in Thee alone, and withdraw it from all creatures; that also our old man, with all the affections thereof, may be daily more and more crucified; and that we may offer up ourselves unto Thee a living sacrifice, to the glory of Thy Holy Name and to the edification of our neighbors, through Jesus Christ our Lord. AMEN.

O MOST Merciful God and Father, we beseech Thee, that Thou wilt be pleased to work in our hearts through the Holy Spirit, that we may daily, more and more, with true confidence, give ourselves up unto Thy Son Jesus Christ: that we may no longer live in our sins, but He in us and we in Him. Grant us also Thy grace, that we may take upon us our cross cheerfully, deny ourselves, confess our Saviour, and in all tribulation with uplifted heads, expect our Lord Jesus Christ from heaven, where He will make our mortal bodies like unto His most glorious body, and take us unto Him in eternity. AMEN.

O LORD God, and merciful Father, knowing that Thou dost not desire the death of a sinner, but that he may turn from his wickedness and live; and that Thy mercy is infinite, which Thou showest unto those who return to Thee; we heartily call upon Thee, trusting in our Mediator Jesus Christ, who is that Lamb of God that taketh away the sins of the world; and we beseech Thee to commiserate our infirmity, forgiving us all our sins for Christ's sake. Wash us in the pure fountain of His blood, that we may become clean and white as snow. Cover our nakedness with His innocence and righteousness, for the glory of Thy name's sake: clear our understanding of all blindness, and our hearts of all hardness and pride; write Thy laws (according to Thy promise) in the tables of our hearts, and strengthen us to delight and walk in the same, to the praise and glory of Thy name, and to the edification of Thy Church. O gracious Father, we ask for, and desire all these things in the name of Jesus Christ. AMEN.

O LORD, forsaking ourselves and all human assistance, we fly for succor to the blessed covenant of grace, by means whereof our Lord Jesus Christ, having offered His body once on the cross as a perfect sacrifice for us, hath reconciled us with Thee forever. Therefore, O Lord, look upon the face of Thine Anointed and not on our sins. And cause Thy face to shine on us to our joy and salvation. Take us henceforth into Thy holy guidance and protection; and govern us by Thy Holy Spirit, who daily, more and more, mortifying our flesh with all its lusts, renews us to a better life. That hereby Thy Name may be glorified and praised to all eternity; and that we, despising all transitory things, may, with an ardent desire, fix our thoughts only on things heavenly, through Jesus Christ our Lord.  AMEN.

O LORD, take us, together with all that belongs to or concerns us, into Thy keeping.  Grant that we may live according to Thy will, and so use the gifts which we receive of Thy blessing, that they may not impede, but rather further us unto life eternal. Strengthen us in all temptations, that we, striving in true faith, may overcome, and hereafter enjoy with Christ life eternal.  We ask these things in the name of our faithful Lord and Saviour Jesus Christ.  AMEN.

O ALMIGHTY God and Merciful Father, grant that we may die unto this world and all earthly things, and that we may daily more and more be renewed after the image of Jesus Christ.  Suffer us not to be separated by any means from Thy love.  But draw us daily nigher and nigher unto Thee, that we may enter upon the end of our calling with joy—may die, rise again, and live with Christ in eternity.  Hear us through Jesus Christ.  AMEN.

STRENGTHEN, O Lord, the ministers of Thy Church, that they may faithfully and steadfastly declare Thy holy word.  Preserve us from all deceit and unfaithfulness.  Confound all evil and subtile counsels taken against Thy word and Church.  Withhold not from us Thy Spirit and word, but grant us increase of faith, and in all trouble and adversity, patience and constancy.  Assist Thy Church.  Deliver her from all affliction, derision, and persecution.  Strengthen also the weak and sorrowful of heart. And send us Thy peace, through Jesus Christ our Lord. AMEN.

ALMIGHTY and Merciful God, bless and long preserve Thy servant the President of the United States, and all placed in authority. Replenish them with all grace and heavenly gifts, that they may wisely govern, and strenuously protect the people whom Thou hast committed to their care, faithfully defend Thy worship, and rightly administer justice; that these United States being preserved from all enemies, the evil-doers punished, and the just protected, Thy Name thereby may be praised, and the kingdom of the King of kings, Christ Jesus, be promoted; and that we may lead quiet and peaceable lives in all godliness and honesty, through Jesus Christ our Lord. AMEN.

MERCIFUL God, we beseech Thee for all those whom Thou dost afflict with poverty, imprisonment, sickness of body, or trouble of mind. Comfort them all according to their several necessities. Grant that their chastisement may bring them to the knowledge of their sins, and to an amendment of their lives. Give them also firm patience. Alleviate their sufferings. And, finally, deliver them, that they may rejoice in Thy goodness and eternally praise Thy Name through Jesus Christ. AMEN.

O MERCIFUL Father, be pleased to forgive all our sins through the holy passion and blood-shedding of our Lord and Saviour Jesus Christ. Enlighten also our hearts that we, having cast off all works of darkness, may as children of light, walk in a new life in all godliness. Bless also the preaching of Thy Gospel. Destroy all works of the devil. Comfort all those who are persecuted and afflicted: Through Jesus Christ Thy beloved Son, who hath promised us that Thou wilt certainly give us whatsoever we shall ask in His name. AMEN.

O MERCIFUL God, Eternal Light shining in darkness, who dispellest the night of sin, enlighten the eyes of our understanding that we may not sleep in death. Defend us against all assaults of the devil, and take us into Thy holy protection. We beseech Thee to hide our sins with Thy mercy, as Thou hidest all things on earth with the darkness of the night. Relieve and comfort all those who are afflicted or distressed in mind, body, or estate, through Jesus Christ our Lord. AMEN.

#### From other Liturgies of the Reformed Churches.

HEAVENLY Father! we give Thee immortal praise and thanks, that upon us poor sinners Thou hast conferred so great a benefit, as to bring us into the communion of Thy Son Jesus Christ our Lord; whom having delivered up to death for us, Thou hast given for our food and nourishment unto eternal life. Now, also, grant us grace, that we may never be unmindful of these things; but rather carrying them about engraven upon our hearts, may advance and grow in that faith which is effectual unto every good work. Thus may the rest of our lives be ordered and followed out to Thy glory and the edification of our neighbors: Through Jesus Christ our Lord;

who with Thee, O Father, and the Holy Ghost, liveth and reigneth in the unity of the Godhead, world without end. AMEN.

BE pleased to have compassion upon us, O most gracious God, Father of all mercies, for the sake of Thy Son Jesus Christ our Lord. And in removing our guilt and our pollution, grant us the daily increase of the grace of Thine Holy Spirit; that acknowledging from our inmost hearts our own unrighteousness, we may be touched with sorrow that shall work true repentance; and that Thy Spirit, mortifying all sin within us, may produce the fruits of holiness and of righteousness well-pleasing in Thy sight: Through Jesus Christ our Lord. AMEN.

MOST gracious God, our heavenly Father, in whom alone dwelleth all fulness of light and wisdom: Illuminate our minds, we beseech Thee, by Thine Holy Spirit, in the true understanding of Thy word. Give us grace, that we may receive it with reverence and humility unfeigned. May it lead us to put our whole trust in Thee alone; and so to serve and honor Thee, that we may glorify Thy holy name, and edify our neighbors by a good example. And since it hath pleased Thee to number us among Thy people, oh! help us to pay Thee the love and homage that we owe, as children to our Father, and as servants to our Lord. We ask this for the sake of our Master and Saviour. AMEN.

O ALMIGHTY God! who alone canst order the unruly wills and affections of sinful men: Grant unto us Thy people, that we may love the things which Thou commandest, and desire that which Thou dost promise; that so, among the sundry and manifold changes of the world, our hearts may surely there be fixed, where true joys are to be found: Through Jesus Christ our Lord. AMEN.

ALMIGHTY and Everlasting God, who of Thy tender love towards mankind hast sent Thy Son, our Saviour Jesus Christ, to take upon Him our flesh, and that in the form of a servant, and to suffer death, even the death of the Cross, for our redemption, and that we should follow the example of His great humility, patience, and obedience: Mercifully grant that this mind may be in us which was also in Christ Jesus, that we may both follow the example of His humble obedience and patient suffering, and also be made partakers of His glorious resurrection, to live with Thee for ever. Grant this for the sake of Thy Son our Saviour Jesus Christ. AMEN.

ALMIGHTY God, give us grace, that we may cast away the works of darkness, and put upon us the armor of light, now in the time of this mortal life, in which Thy Son Jesus Christ came to visit us with great humility: that in the last day, when He shall come again in His glorious Majesty to judge both the quick and the dead, we may rise to the life immortal: Through Him who liveth and reigneth with Thee and the Holy Ghost, now and ever. AMEN.

O LORD, who hast given us cause of perpetual joy by the coming of Thy Son our Saviour among us:

Raise up Thy power, we pray Thee, and possess us with a mighty sense of Thy wonderful love; that whereas through the cares of this life we are sorely let and hindered in running the race that is set before us, we may be careful for nothing, but thankfully commending ourselves in every thing to Thy bountiful grace and mercy, the peace of Thee our God, which passeth all understanding, may keep our hearts and minds, through the satisfaction of Thy Son our Lord, to whom, with Thee and the Holy Ghost, be honor and glory, world without end. AMEN.

ALMIGHTY God, who hast given Thine only Son to be unto us both a sacrifice for sin, and also an example of godly life: Give us grace that we may always most thankfully receive that His most inestimable benefit; and also daily endeavor to follow the blessed steps of His most holy life: that dying unto sin, and living unto righteousness, we may at last obtain eternal life: Through the same Jesus Christ our Lord. AMEN.

BLESSED Lord, whose only Son our Saviour Jesus Christ hath once suffered for our sins, the just for the unjust, that He might bring us to Thee our God: We beseech Thee, that as we are baptized into His death, so by continually mortifying our corrupt affections we may be buried with Him; and at last through the grave, and gate of death, pass to our joyful resurrection: For His merits, who died, and was buried, and rose again, Thy Son Jesus Christ our Lord. AMEN.

GRANT, we beseech Thee, Almighty God, that the words which we have heard this day with our outward ears, may, through Thy grace, be so grafted inwardly in our hearts, that they may bring forth in us the fruit of good living; to the honor and praise of Thy Name: Through Jesus Christ our Lord. AMEN.

O GOD, Holy Ghost, Sanctifier of the Faithful, visit, we pray Thee, this congregation with Thy love and favor; enlighten their minds more and more with the light of the everlasting Gospel; graft in their hearts a love of the truth; increase in them true religion; nourish them with all goodness; and of Thy great mercy keep them in the same, O blessed Spirit: Whom, with the Father and the Son, together we worship and glorify as one God, world without end. AMEN.

# Ancient Hymns

### AND

## Selections from Scripture for Chanting.

---

#### DOXOLOGY.

GLORY be to the Father, and to the Son, and to the Holy Ghost;

As it was in the beginning, is now, and ever shall be, world without end. AMEN.

#### TERSANCTUS.

IT is very meet, right, and our bounden duty, that we should at all times, and in all places, give thanks unto Thee, O Lord, Holy Father, Almighty, Everlasting God.

Therefore with Angels and Archangels, and with all the company of heaven, we laud and magnify Thy glorious Name; evermore praising Thee, and saying, Holy, holy, holy, Lord God of Sabaoth, heaven and earth are full of Thy glory: Glory be to Thee, O Lord most High. AMEN.

## TE DEUM LAUDAMUS.

We praise thee, O God, we acknowledge thee to be the Lord.

All the earth doth worship thee, the Father everlasting.

To thee all angels cry aloud, the Heavens, and all the Powers therein.

To thee Cherubim, and Seraphim, continually do cry,

Holy, holy, holy, Lord God of Sabaoth;

Heaven and earth are full of the majesty of Thy glory.

The glorious company of the Apostles praise Thee.

The goodly fellowship of the Prophets praise Thee.

The noble army of Martyrs praise Thee.

The holy Church throughout all the world, doth acknowledge Thee;

The Father, of an infinite majesty;

Thine adorable, true, and only Son;

Also the Holy Ghost, the Comforter.

Thou art the King of Glory, O Christ.

Thou art the everlasting Son, of the Father.

When Thou tookest upon Thee to deliver man, Thou didst humble Thyself to be born of a Virgin.

When Thou hadst overcome the sharpness of death, Thou didst open the kingdom of Heaven to all believers.

Thou sittest at the right hand of God, in the Glory of the Father.

We believe that Thou shalt come, to be our Judge.

We therefore pray Thee, help Thy servants, whom Thou hast redeemed with Thy precious blood.

Make them to be numbered with Thy Saints, in glory everlasting.

O Lord, save Thy people, and bless Thine heritage.

Govern them, and lift them up for ever.

Day by day, we magnify Thee;

And we worship Thy Name, ever, world without end.

Vouchsafe, O Lord, to keep us this day without sin.

O Lord, have mercy upon us, have mercy upon us.

O Lord, let Thy mercy be upon us, as our trust is in Thee.

O Lord, in Thee have I trusted, let me never be confounded.

### BENEDICTUS.

Blessed be the Lord God of Israel;
For He hath visited and redeemed His people.

And hath raised up a mighty salvation for us;
In the house of His servant David.

As He spake by the mouth of His holy prophets;
Which have been since the world began.

That we should be saved from our enemies;
And from the hand of all that hate us.

### BONUM EST.

It is a good thing to give thanks unto the Lord:
And to sing praise unto Thy name, O Most Highest.

To tell of Thy loving-kindness early in the morning:
And of Thy truth in the night season.

Upon an instrument of ten strings, and upon the lute:
Upon a loud instrument, and upon the harp.

For Thou Lord, hast made me glad through Thy works:
And I will rejoice in giving praise for the operations of Thy hands.

### PSALM XXIII.

The Lord is my Shepherd;
I shall not want.

He maketh me to lie down in green pastures;
He leadeth me beside the still waters.

He restoreth my soul;
He leadeth me in the paths of righteousness for His name's sake.

Yea though I walk through the valley of the shadow of death, I will fear no evil;
For Thou art with me, Thy rod and Thy staff they comfort me.

Thou preparest a table before me in the presence of mine enemies;
Thou anointest my head with oil, my cup runneth over.

Surely goodness and mercy shall follow me all the days of my life;
And I will dwell in the house of the Lord for ever.

## PSALM LI.

Have mercy upon me, O God, according to Thy loving-kindness:
According unto the multitude of Thy tender mercies blot out my transgressions.

Wash me thoroughly from mine iniquity;
And cleanse me from my sin.

For I acknowledge my transgressions;
And my sin is ever before me.

Hide Thy face from my sins;
And blot out all mine iniquities.

Create in me a clean heart, O God;
And renew a right spirit within me.

Cast me not away from Thy presence;
And take not Thy Holy Spirit from me.

Restore unto me the joy of Thy salvation;
And uphold me with Thy free Spirit.

Then will I teach transgressors Thy ways;
And sinners shall be converted unto Thee.

O Lord, open Thou my lips;
And my mouth shall show forth Thy praise.

For Thou desirest not sacrifice, else would I give it;
Thou delightest not in burnt-offering.

The sacrifices of God are a broken spirit;
A broken and a contrite heart, O God, Thou wilt not despise.

## PSALM LXVII.

God be merciful unto us and bless us;
And cause His face to shine upon us.

That Thy way may be known upon earth;
Thy saving health among all nations.

Let the people praise Thee, O God;
Let all the people praise Thee.

O let the nations be glad and sing for joy;
For Thou shalt judge the people righteously, and govern the nations upon earth.

Let the people praise Thee, O God;
Let all the people praise Thee.

Then shall the earth yield her increase;
And God, even our own God, shall bless us.

God shall bless us;
And all the ends of the earth shall fear Him.

## PSALM XCVIII.

O come, let us sing unto the Lord;
Let us heartily rejoice in the strength of our salvation.

Let us come before His presence with thanksgiving;
And show ourselves glad in Him with psalms.

For the Lord is a great God;
And a great King above all gods.

In His hands are all the corners of the earth;
And the strength of the hills is His also.

The sea is His, and He made it;
And His hands prepared the dry land.

O come, let us worship and fall down;
And kneel before the Lord our Maker.

For He is the Lord our God;
And we are the people of His pasture and the sheep of His hand.

O worship the Lord in the beauty of holiness;
Let the whole earth stand in awe of Him.

For He cometh, for He cometh to judge the earth;
And with righteousness to judge the world, and the people with His truth.

### PSALM C.

O be joyful in the Lord, all ye lands;
Serve the Lord with gladness, and come before His presence with a song.

Be ye sure that the Lord He is God;
It is He that hath made us and not we ourselves, we are His people, and the sheep of His pasture.

O go your way into His gates with thanksgiving, and into His courts with praise;
Be thankful unto Him and speak good of His name.

For the Lord is gracious, His mercy is everlasting;
And His truth endureth from generation to generation.

### PSALM CIII.

Bless the Lord, O my soul:
And all that is within me, bless His holy name.

Bless the Lord, O my soul:
And forget not all His benefits.

Who forgiveth all thine iniquities:
Who healeth all thy diseases.

Who redeemeth thy life from destruction:
Who crowneth thee with loving-kindness and tender mercies.

Bless the Lord, ye His angels, that excel in strength:
That do His commandments, hearkening unto the voice of His word.

Bless ye the Lord, all ye His hosts:
Ye ministers of His, that do His pleasure.

Bless the Lord, all His works, in all places of His dominion:
Bless the Lord, O my soul.

### PSALM CXXX.

Out of the depths;
Have I cried unto Thee, O Lord.

Lord, hear my voice;
Let Thine ears be attentive to the voice of my supplications.

If Thou, Lord, shouldest mark iniquities;
O Lord, who shall stand?

But there is forgiveness with Thee;
That Thou mayest be feared.

I wait for the Lord, my soul doth wait;
And in His word do I hope.

My soul waiteth for the Lord more than they that watch for the morning;
  I say more than they that watch for the morning.

Let Israel hope in the Lord;
  For with the Lord there is mercy, and with Him is plenteous redemption.

And He shall redeem Israel;
  From all his iniquities.

### ISAIAH LIII.

He is despised and rejected of men;
  A man of sorrows, and acquainted with grief.

And we hid as it were our faces from Him;
  He was despised, and we esteemed Him not.

Surely He hath borne our griefs and carried our sorrows;
  Yet we did esteem Him stricken, smitten of God, and afflicted.

But He was wounded for our transgressions;
  He was bruised for our iniquities.

The chastisement of our peace was upon Him;
  And with His stripes we are healed.

All we like sheep have gone astray;
  We have turned every one to his own way.

And the Lord hath laid on Him;
  The iniquity of us all.

BAPTISMAL.

###### To follow the Thanksgiving after Baptism.

Then will I sprinkle clean water upon you;
And ye shall be clean.

A new heart also will I give you;
And a new spirit will I put within you.

And I will take away the stony heart out of your flesh;
And I will give you a heart of flesh.

And I will put my Spirit within you;
And ye shall keep my judgments, and do them.

And they brought young children to Him, that He should touch them;
And His disciples rebuked those that brought them.

But when Jesus saw it He was much displeased;
And said unto them, Suffer the little children to come unto me, and forbid them not, for of such is the kingdom of God.

Verily, I say unto you;
Whosoever shall not receive the kingdom of God as a little child he shall not enter therein.

And He took them up in His arms;
Put His hands upon them and blessed them.

AMEN.

## Responses to the Decalogue.

### I.

Lord have mercy upon us, and write all these Thy laws in our hearts, we beseech Thee. Amen.

### II.

Thy word is a lamp unto my feet;
And a light unto my path.
How sweet are Thy words unto my taste;
Yea, sweeter than honey to my mouth.
Give me understanding, and I will keep Thy law,
For therein do I delight, O Lord my God. Amen.

### III.

\* O Lord God, merciful Father!

Deign so to write Thy law on our hearts by Thy Spirit:

That in our life hereafter;

We may wish and choose nothing more, than by complete obedience, to please Thee in all things, through Jesus Christ Thy Son. Amen.

\* From the Liturgy of Pollanus, A.D. 1546, with which this usage of response to the Decalogue originated.

# Historical Note.

By the courtesy of Rev. Charles W. Baird we give, from his admirable work entitled Eutaxia, or The Presbyterian Liturgies, the early history of the Liturgy of the Reformed Dutch Church.

As it now stands, the Reformed Dutch Liturgy is, we believe, precisely what it was in the year 1619, and substantially as when first adopted in 1568. The greater part of its forms indeed date back to the year 1541, and like almost every thing else in the ritual of the Reformed Churches, must be ascribed to the great Reformer Calvin.

A brief history of the compilation of this Liturgy may not be without interest to the reader. For the leading facts here given, we are indebted to the systematic and reliable work of the German ritualist Ebrard.

In 1541, if not earlier, Calvin composed for the congregation to which he had ministered awhile at Strasburgh, a form of worship, which was printed in 1545 at that city. This formulary resembled closely his Liturgy of Geneva, but seems to have contained some features not to be found in the latter. It lies at the foundation of the Dutch and German Reformed rituals, and, as we have had occasion to notice elsewhere, was the source of several portions of the English Book of Common Prayer.

In 1546 Valerandus Pollanus, successor of Calvin as minister of the congregation at Strasburgh, published a liturgy for his people, which appears to have been identical with Calvin's. For in 1551, having passed over with his flock to England, where they established themselves at Glastonbury, in Somersetshire, Pollanus published "a translation of Calvin's Liturgy of Strasburgh," as it was used by his congregation. It was this version which was used by Cranmer and his colleagues in drawing up the Common Prayer-Book.

Shortly after this publication, A Lasco, the distinguished superintendent of the German and Walloon congregations, which had been formed at London, prepared in Latin a liturgy on the basis of that which Pollanus had translated from Calvin; and this composes the substance of the Holland Liturgy, as well as that of the Palatinate.

A Lasco's liturgy, thus founded on Pollanus's translation, was rendered into the Dutch language in 1556 by John Utenhoven, an eminent Christian layman of the period. The Latin edition meanwhile was published at Frankfort in 1555, entitled, "The Form of Ecclesiastical Service in the German Church of Foreigners, established at London, in England."

But before this, in 1554, an abridgment of A Lasco's yet unpublished liturgy had been made by Martin Micronius; and this was printed in the Dutch language at Embden, in Hanover, under the title, "Christian Ordinances of the Netherlands Congregations of CHRIST, with the Approbation of the Ministers and Elders of the Church of CHRIST of the Low Dutch at London. Diligently corrected and arranged by Martin Micronius."

A few farther modifications brought this formulary into its present shape. Composed originally by Calvin in French, translated by Pollanus into the English, rearranged by A Lasco in Latin, then translated by Utenhoven into the Dutch, and abridged by Micronius, it was finally reviewed by Dathenus, and adopted in 1556 as the standard of worship in the Reformed Church of Holland.

Some of the offices are of more modern date. The "Consolation of the Sick" was introduced in 1587, and the form of baptizing adults in 1604.

The numerous congregations of refugees from Holland which were formed in England during the Spanish persecution of that country, used this order of worship. At one period of the reign of Queen Elizabeth there were no fewer than eight congregations of Dutch Protestants in the city of London alone. The number diminished, however, before many years, and for more than a century there existed but one such congregation, now, we believe, entirely extinct.

The forms of worship of the Holland churches, which were observed in London, as well as at other towns in England, with the full approbation and sanction of the Anglican Reformers, commended themselves, by their Scriptural purity and beauty, to the respect of all Protestant communions; and it is a curious fact, recorded in the history of the Huguenots, that when about the middle of the eighteenth century all assemblies for worship, according to the rites of the French Reformed Church, were forbidden, the Protestants of Paris were accustomed to meet and celebrate divine service after the forms of the Church of Holland, by which course they evaded the letter of the law, and at the same time beautifully exemplified the harmony of these sister Churches in their doctrines and ordinances.

The Liturgy of the Reformed Dutch Church was first translated into English for the use of several English and Scottish congregations formed in Holland. The translation now in use was effected toward the latter part of the past century by the Rev. Dr. Livingston, and is remarkably faithful and correct.

# Ancient Usages.

The following extracts from Chapter VII. of the "History and Characteristics of the Reformed Protestant Dutch Church," by the Rev. Dr. Demarest, now Professor in the Theological Seminary at New-Brunswick, N. J., furnish interesting information as to the ancient usages of the Reformed Dutch Churches. This reliable and attractive book will abundantly repay a careful perusal.

On the accession of Edward VI. to the throne of England, the eyes of the Reformed of every land were turned to that country. Many went thither from the Netherlands, and among them a number of members from the church of Embden, who founded a church in Austin Friars, London. This was under the care of A Lasco and four other ministers, and is in existence at the present day. The British reformers took great interest in these refugees, and A Lasco, who was of a noble Polish family, and a bishop in Hungary, came over by express invitation of Cranmer, and was made by the King superintendent of the foreign Protestants who had fled to England.

Forms of worship were at once prepared by A Lasco, for the use of the church in London, and subsequently Pollanus, the successor of Calvin, at Strasburg, came with his congregation to England, and having settled at Glastonbury, published a translation of the liturgy which Calvin had prepared for their use in the French language. A Lasco now prepared a new liturgy for the London church, using their old one, and also the translation of the Strasburg Litany by Pollanus. This was written in Latin, and corresponds in its outlines with our present Liturgy.

The following description of the order of worship in the church of London has been translated from an old Dutch author, by Rev. Dr. De Witt: "The congregation being assembled in their house of worship, the minister ascended the pulpit and commenced with a brief exhortation to the solemn and devout observance of worship. Prayer was then offered according to a prescribed form, the same which is still found in our Liturgy, with the title, 'A Prayer before the Explanation of the Catechism.' After this a Psalm was sung. The minister then preached on a portion of Scripture, commonly consisting not of one, two, or three verses, but of a continuous paragraph, or a history standing by itself. Thus the minister illustrated, explained, and enforced a whole book of Scripture—as, for instance, the Epistle to the Romans—in continuance. The sermon or homily occupied about an hour. After this the minister announced what was proper to be announced to the congregation, but only that which respected public worship. After this a prayer was again offered, according to a prescribed form, which was short and very appropriate. The ten commandments were then distinctly and emphatically read, after which the minister exhorted the congregation to confession of sin, and then offered prayer in penitent confession of sin, and supplication for divine forgiveness, according to a prescribed form, brief and impressive. After this he read the following declaration: 'Seeing it pleases God to receive in his grace those who are truly penitent and sincerely confess their sins, and, on the contrary, to leave obstinate sinners, who cover and palliate their sins, to themselves, I therefore declare, from the Word of God, to the penitent who believe in Christ alone for salvation, that through his merits alone their sins are forgiven of God. Amen. And to as many as do not confess and forsake their sins, or who, if they confess their sins, seek salvation from any other source than the merits and grace of Christ, and thus love darkness rather than light, I declare, from the Word of God, that their sins are bound in heaven until they repent and turn to Christ.' Immediately after this the Apostles' Creed was read, as bearing the common confession of their faith. Then followed the long or general prayer, either in the prescribed form of the liturgy, or else, at the discretion of the minister, accommodated to the wants and circumstances of the church. The prayers were concluded with the Lord's Prayer. A psalm was then sung by the whole congregation, led by a chorister placed in front, near the pulpit.

The minister then commended the wants of the poor to the alms of the brethren, which were collected by the deacons at the door of the church, after the dismission of the congregation. The benediction was pronounced in the form, 'The Lord bless you,'" etc.

Slight changes from this order were made in Holland. The clerk or voorleser standing in the baptistery, (doophuisje,) under the pulpit, opened the services by reading a few texts of Scripture, then the ten commandments, and a chapter, and then he read a psalm, and led in singing it; tablets were hung on the walls, indicating the Psalm to be sung. During the singing the minister appeared, and having stood a few moments at the foot of the pulpit-stairs in silent prayer, he entered the pulpit. Then followed a few remarks, bearing on what was to be the subject of discourse. This was called the "exordium remotum." Then followed prayer, which was according to form or not, at discretion; then the sermon, which, in early times was an expository lecture in course. At first the Apostles' Creed was read after the sermon, but in later times it was used only in the afternoon service. The sermon in the afternoon was an exposition of one of the Lord's days of the Heidelberg Catechism.

The same order essentially was for many years observed in this country.

The customs of the Church, in reference to the administration of the sacraments, afford materials of interesting history. It has been stated that in the churches first formed in the Netherlands, no children were baptized but those of members in full communion; but that afterward the privilege was extended to the children of such baptized persons as were of good moral character. It is optional with consistories among us to adopt whichever mode they think proper.

This sacrament was formerly administered after sermon, now generally before it. Sponsors used to be associated with the parents. Baptized children were claimed to be under the particular care of the Church, which, in connection with the parents, attended to their religious training.

The sacrament of the Lord's Supper was at the first observed every two months. Candidates for membership met at the minister's house, and the preparatory service was held a few days before the communion.

On the communion Sabbath, after the usual services, the form was read, and the minister and as many of the members as could, seated themselves at the table before the pulpit. These, having partaken of the elements, gave way for others, until the whole church had communed. In the intervals, portions of Scripture were read by the clerk, or an elder. At first, the elders served at the table, but this duty was afterward transferred to the deacons. In the earliest period, in Holland, the communicants, before approaching the table, fell on their knees in their places, and looking upward, offered silent prayer.

The writer has a distinct remembrance of the manner in which the Lord's Supper was celebrated under the ministry of Rev. James V. C. Romeyn, at Hackensack and Schraalenberg. The communicants stood at the table, the aged male members taking precedence, and who, on retiring, were followed by their younger brethren. The females followed in the same order. Last of all the colored members approached the table. The minister broke the bread as he passed round the table, giving to each one his portion from his own hand, and accompanying it with some remark or quotation from Scripture, often beautifully adapted to the particular case. While the communicants were retiring, and others taking their places at the table, a verse from a hymn was sung.

The churches in the Netherlands, and also for a long time in this country, observed the feasts of Christmas, Easter, and Whit-Sunday, commemorative of the birth and resurrection of the Saviour, and of the outpouring of the Holy Spirit on the day of Pentecost. In addition to these, the circumcision and ascension of Christ were commemorated in many churches, and it was customary to celebrate the Sacrament of the Lord's Supper on Christmas-day and Easter Sunday.

www.ingramcontent.com/pod-product-compliance
Lightning Source LLC
Chambersburg PA
CBHW032243080426
42735CB00008B/979